i

THE PERFECT LOVE BOOK

THE PERFECT LOVE BOOK

Cover Design by MADDCity MEDIA

Website: .http://shop.ndbrennanauthor.com

This book was originally published by arrangement with MADDCity MEDIA.

N. D. Brennan, Authors

THE PERFECT LOVE BOOK / N.D. Brennan - Second Edition

1. Romance 2. Love 3. Relationship
4. Christian 5. Marriage 6. Couples I. N. D. "Indy" Brennan, author II. Title

ISBN-13: 97-98849627878

Published by arrangement with MADDCity.Live, LLC and MADDCity Media.

Typeset Arial

"I sleep, but my heart waketh: it is the voice of my beloved that knocketh, saying, open to me, my sister, my love, my dove, my undefiled: for my head is filled with dew, and my locks with the drops of the night."

Song of Solomon 5:2

N. D. "Indy" Brennan

PREFACE

This book is a guide for married couples, engaged couples, and for people who aspire to ultimately achieve the perfect loving union. One of the most beautiful terms regarding a covenant relationship between a man and a woman is to "cover." Whenever I think of this expression, I instantly picture being at war and someone jumping in front and taking a bullet for me. The Bible says that Jesus laid down His own life (John 10:18) as a sacrifice for sin so that those who believe in Him would not perish but would have eternal life.

A close friend reminded me recently of a principle practiced by famed real estate developer J. Massey and bestselling author Grant Cordone. Each man, when discussing how to protect their family from corruption, admitted refraining from outside activities that tend to invite problems into relationships. They went as far as suggesting they avoided engaging with certain people and parties as a preventative measure for ensuring the focus within their marriage. This type of responsible conduct is also a form of "covering." In a manner of speaking, they take the necessary steps to avoid anything that may compromise or harm their relationship with their wives as well as their wives themselves.

Author David Cross defines "God's covering" as an expression which describes the spiritual protection and nurture which God provides for all those who are in a covenant relationship with Him. Within this book, I reference that special man or woman who God has designated to be your wife or husband as "The One." For a man in particular, the greatest gift God has ever given us, excluding life itself and Christ, is "the woman." Allow me to stress that I'm not referring to any and every woman who may happen to step into our lives from time to time. I'm referring very specifically to that one woman that God created in order to perfect the greatness that is your life. This is "The One" who He has also given you the courage to enjoy what this book refers to as "The Perfect Love."

Inasmuch, it is the responsibility of each member of your covenant relationship to "cover" each other. Making this plain, it's about taking the necessary steps to ensure the emotional, psychological, physical, and spiritual confidence, stability, and safety of your partner, mate, or spouse. For many of us who have been through the fire in various relationships and gone through enough storms, "covering" your partner or spouse is practically a no-brainer. It is our responsibility to do as God does for us for each other. If we are to be like Him, one of our primary objectives is to ensure spiritual protection while continuing to nurture our mate.

"Covering your wife" is a physical declaration stating, "I will take a bullet for you before I allow any harm or hurt to come to you." It's about understanding and appreciating the gift you have been given.

The "Perfect Love" is a book written to assist you in finding your way through the various relationships and giving into God's direction and influence. This book also provides instruction on methods for maintaining and sustaining your "perfect love" once you've found "The One." The "Perfect Love" is about complete honesty and openness with each other, which results in a degree of freedom that you may never have previously experienced. But it's also about avoiding the challenges, pitfalls, and temptations that may occasionally attempt to breach your covenant.

Understand that within "The Perfect Love," God has connected you with the missing piece of your life's puzzle, even if you didn't realize it wasn't finished.

It is my prayer that this book will help to enlighten and encourage you to embrace the life that God desires for you. May your everyday be as He intended: A perfect life through a perfect love.

THE PERFECT LOVE POEM

She is my poetry's refrain.
My destiny's determination to distance me from what...
...is supposed to be.
She is my 3-lines and 17 syllables,
My iambic pentameter, the misuse of my prose,
And the subject matter to every spoken word.

One moment with her is like
Going around the world
15 times within 15 seconds
On the backs of fairies' wings
And the friends of my enemies.

Whew...
She leaves me breathless

Causing me to crave for the stimulation
inspired by a singular exhalation;
As she breathes out,
I breathe in,
Again and again and again...

What she leaves out,
I take in.
For I am pre-consumed
By the divine predisposition
That she is everything I am supposed to be.
She is everything I could never be...
... alone.

TABLE OF CONTENTS

N. D. "Indy" Brennan

CHAPTER ONE
WHAT IS "THE PERFECT LOVE"?

N. D. "Indy" Brennan

What is the "Perfect Love?"

"And they were both naked, the man and his wife, and they were not ashamed." (Genesis 2:25).

The question is: How or Why?

Answer: *"Love dispels fear because fear focuses on punishment and won't let love mature. The one who is afraid of God does not understand God's love."* (1 John 4:18 – The Clear Work translation).

These two verses fall squarely at the heart of this book. When brought together, the result symbolizes what is both proscribed and prescribed within a *"perfect love."* Together, these two references wonderfully identify what the expectation should be between a husband and a wife. The perfect love is the flawless reflection of the perfectness of God's eternal love for us.

You see…the perfect love is an unbreakable, boundless, unconditional, and longing affection between a man and his wife. This bond is appointed and anointed by God just for the two of them, establishing a unique wholeness of life. Most of all, this is a bond that is to be shared exclusively between the two of them, creating a singular new creation in Christ. It is through this bond that the two are covered by an impermeable and unblemished seal of protection by God. In a word, the two transform into a version of utter perfection.

If that isn't enough…. The perfect love represents a peace that surpasses all understanding and the substance of everything one could ever hope or imagine. It's the culmination of two individual lives fused suddenly into one, manifesting a virtually new physical existence. In turn, this new presence of life empowers you with the ability to rise above any challenge, shortcoming, or pitfall you otherwise would have faced alone. But it also provides you with a greater reason to celebrate newfound celebrity, success, or accomplishment. In truth, the *"perfect love"* is beyond the acceptability or comprehension of most, unless or until…

I want to invite you to imagine for a moment suddenly finding your very best friend. I'm not talking about the euphemism defining someone that you are somewhat *"close to"* or that you may have known for years. And I'm definitely not referring to that person who you are *"permanently"* attached until something unexpected or unprecedented occurs. No. The person I'm describing is a person who accepts you and all your flaws. This is a person who remains there beside you regardless of the error of your ways and any hurt you may have caused deeply. This person sticks with you regardless of whatever ugliness may happen in your life. Regardless of *"whatever,"* this person remains there, eagerly awaiting your call and ready to encourage you even when you didn't know you needed it. This is the one person who proves that love has not left you despite the negative turn your life may have taken and the abandonment of others.

This is a person who you can confidently disclose your most intimate secrets and reveal your most disappointing, detestable, and normally unforgivable acts or thoughts. This person extends constructive criticism intended to lift you up even if it feels as if their words are tearing you down. This person hears your heart without judgment. The fact is a real best friendship borders on the supernatural because most would not believe it possible, especially between a man and a woman.

Uniquely, the existence of this very exceptional being inspires a degree of confidence and comfort that may feel new, surreal, or unfamiliar. This is a person who tirelessly and lovingly continues to care for you as if no time was ever lost and no harm has ever been committed. The *"perfect love"* exposes a person who unequivocally believes in you and who celebrates your mere potential. They appear to never lose sight of how wonderful you are regardless of how you may question yourself or the adverse perception of others. This person is an unyielding reminder of the great things you deserve in life despite what even you may otherwise suggest.

Now, imagine knowing that regardless of whatever you may go through, regardless of wherever you may go, or wherever life may lead you, that individual…that best friend…turns out to sincerely always be there for you. Imagine that person remaining an unrelenting ear for you to confide. But not only that. Here's a person who God has given you to share your worst as well as your best. This is a person who you could spend the rest of your life with and offer every drip-drop of your heart with confidence. Imagine this person living to breathe every breath you exhale and who adores you beyond measure. This is a person with the audacity to love you as much as you desire to love them.

Now…. Imagine this amazing individual being your husband or wife with nothing between the two of you but life and love. Imagine sharing a lifetime with this very special individual where no lies, no secrets, and no fear exists. This is the *"perfect love…"*

You see, that's what God has prepared for you. This is what you are entitled as a child of God. And this is what is discovered when you are fortunate enough to find and connect with *"the one."* This is the life great authors write about and great movies depict. It is a life where the two of you are wonderfully forged into a single, unified existence.

The *"perfect love"* is much greater than the most fantastic imagination of legendary filmmakers or your most prolific storytellers. The *"perfect love"* exceeds what most would even dare to dream. While fantasy and fiction are great, the *"perfect love"* personifies a living, breathing reality. And that reality is *"God."*

It doesn't take a rocket scientist to deduce that the life of most people does not conclude where one is living the life of a *"perfect love."* In most instances, couples resign to their separate corners when things become too extreme or difficult. While there are those isolated occurrences where people make it through, people grow apart or simply walk away from a marriage relationship more often than one could count.

Some use the excuse that they have changed. Some nimbly avoid relationship potholes for years just to come to a dramatic and epic ending. The fact is almost 50% of marriages in the United States will end in divorce or separation, and there are possibly a million "common" and uncommon reasons why relationships from marriages and engagements fail. But what is described in this book transcends what others consider *"common"* because "the perfect love" is not typical. The "perfect love" is special. The perfect love is God, and *"the one who is afraid of God does not understand God's love."* (1 John 4:118 -The Clear Word translation).

You see, the reality is that there are two things in the world that you can always depend on: Life, as in the case of most people, changes, but God remains the same. And therein lies the key: *"God is love"* (1 John 4:8), and *"his love is perfected in us."* (1 John 4:12). He is what makes the difference!

As the earlier verse read, *"There is NO fear [or shame] in love."* (1 John 4:18 - KJV). Adam and Eve were open to *"getting naked"* and "unashamed" because there was nothing unknown between them.

N. D. "Indy" Brennan

CHAPTER TWO
GETTING NAKED AND BEING UNASHAMED

N. D. "Indy" Brennan

Getting Naked and Being Unashamed

"And they were both naked, the man and his wife, and they were not ashamed." (Genesis 2:25).

When I used to read this scripture, I would often envision what I believe is pictured in the minds of most people: Adam and Eve laying out on this beautiful grassy meadow. The meadow would be surrounded by a host of incredibly tall trees and vibrantly colored flowers. And all of this would be located at the very center of the Garden of Eden. The two would be stark naked. Adam's front would rest ever-so-gently behind Eve as he held her lovingly. Yet, both would be sound asleep and at perfect peace.

Now, the image in your head may not be the exact same as mine. But I'd wager it's probably a similar set of circumstances and surroundings. And regardless of how the picture in our minds may vary, there is always one consistency: They are physically *"naked."* In fact, clothing is not even an option. Everything is exposed. At least, up until the forbidden fruit incident.

The word *"unashamed"* on the other hand simply means that neither Adam nor Eve harbored any insecurities or shame about their nakedness in front of the other. It was more than simply being confident in how they felt about their own body in their individual nakedness. They were most comfortable because of what one was to the other. God created them specifically for each other. They were sharing a life together where no lies, secrets, or fear existed. It was a perfect love.

In the abstract, some may consider the fact that they were confident exposing their naked bodies to one another as a form of "true love." And technically, the love between a husband and a wife "should" be so ingrained that safety, security, confidence, and comfort are innate. One "should" adore the other to a degree that exposure to the other's nakedness is celebrated and honored. And in turn, the other "should" be led to feel so set apart from anyone else that inhibitions, embarrassment, fear, and insecurity are instantly gone. In a "true love" scenario, one's imperfections "should" attribute to the unique flawlessness and perfection in the eyes of the other. The desire for one another "should" be boundless and insatiable. Remember, you're God's gift to each other. Sounds nice right?

Well, here's the thing. While this is an awesome interpretation, this sensibility only scratches the surface of the "perfect love" God desires for a husband and a wife to experience for a lifetime. Understanding the scriptural reference at the beginning of this chapter is established only when a man and a woman collectively understand that this type of love is founded on the power of God convening your confidence in being completely "naked and unashamed" with each other, regardless of what you may be wearing or not wearing at the time.

"Love dispels fear because fear focuses on punishment and won't let love mature." (1 John 4:18).

When one is made to feel uncomfortable, unappreciated, unworthy, or inadequate by his wife or her husband, that hurt typifies a form of "punishment" to the one suffering those feelings. The Word of God clearly explains that pure and true love brings about comfort. It inspires appreciation, adoration, respect, and even peace. So, if one truly understands the rare gift God has given them in his wife or her husband, these types of negative and hurtful emotions should never be intentionally provoked by the other. At least not within the realm of a "perfect love" God establishes.

But therein lies the first fear. There is a fear of heartbreak, infidelity, ridicule, abuse, lying, and sharing your very personal thoughts or feeling online. No one wants to be hurt or disappointed again. And it is these types of fears that often impede the gift God is attempting to give to both of you in being completely "naked and unashamed."

"Be ye angry, and sin not: Let not the sun go down upon your wrath." (Ephesians 4:26).

I'm not here to sell you an impossible dream. So, while the two have become a new singular creation in Christ, that does not mean the two will never disagree. But here's the thing. Many people see disagreements as a negative, and if you are of this common mindset your union may experience similar challenges. But I challenge you to consider this: Within a business deal, a personal relationship, or in the process of developing anything, a positive outcome represents the convergence of an array of varying ideas, experiences, and traditional belief systems. Debates may become passionate. But the key is for the two to remember they are embarking on a degree of perfection that will be unlike any other. Remember that the merger you are forging is specific just to the two of you. And when you both adopt this way of thinking, suddenly debates transform into another building block towards ensuring your "perfect love."

But let's say emotions become slightly higher than normal. It happens. As a preventative measure, an agreement should be established from the very beginning of your engagement or marriage journey. Let disagreements and heightened emotions fade with the setting of the sun. At the end of the day, agree to let it go. Life is too short to allow adversities to disrupt your collective perfection.

Remember, the only two people with the capacity to chink the armor of what God has brought together is one or the two of you. So, when the two of you together don't mind, there is nothing in this world that can be thrown at you that will ultimately matter. It's about uncovering reasons to laugh for example when times appear to be at their most challenging because, at the end of the day, you each recognize "we have us." This strength rises out of the fires forging what God has established in the perfection of your connection.

One definition Webster uses to define the word "naked" is to be "without covering." And again, this description tends to inspire a very specific and consistent mental image leaning into the direction of a person being unclothed or (as the late Bernie Mack would say) "buck naked." But where many miss the mark regarding this expression is where this expression is limited to the idea of physical nakedness. In a biblical sense, "naked" carries a much more profound meaning than this commonly applied minimalization.

For example, to be "naked" is to be fully exposed. This means that nothing is hidden, and everything is unveiled from one to another within your marriage or engagement relationship. A type of "exchange" takes place. The fact is that if this was limited merely to the physical body, a great number of people would find this acceptable. But again, we're talking about the uniqueness of the "perfect love."

Within the "perfect love, being naked "covers" everything that makes up each one of these two very special individuals. This includes his or her past and present, meaning the good and the bad, for better or for worse. And this covers you emotionally as well as physically, intellectually, and yes, to a great extent, even spiritually. Through the power of this love appropriated by God, every area or remote idea about that man or woman is collectively appreciated and adored by her husband or his wife wholly and completely. This is because you perfect or have been perfected for each other. You make each other whole and complete within the perfect love. In an expression, you each represent the one missing piece of a beautifully arranged jigsaw puzzle.

Let's look at Adam and Eve again for example. Some may believe that Adam was made incomplete, imperfect, or flawed when God removed the physical rib from his chest to create Eve. But what God understood within His infinite wisdom, even before Adam realized it, was that Adam was incomplete or "imperfect" long before the rib was ever taken.

Within Adam, God saw a void or a missing piece, which is often the case for many of us. Within our limited exposure and knowledge, we convince ourselves that we are fine and that "life couldn't be better." On some great and powerful level, God must find our ignorance hilarious. When you really think about it, we have not lived long enough or broad enough, especially alone (meaning before connecting to or having a life outside of the "One"), to have the capacity to even envision the full magnitude of all that life has to offer.

What's interesting is Adam possibly felt this way himself. He resided in a virtual haven, seated at the foot of God Himself. And even with all of this before him, it was impossible for Adam to fully understand the even greater life experience God envisioned for him. It was beyond Adam's intellectual capacity to even envision anything greater for his life. Yet, he had only experienced a mere fraction of God's ultimate vision for him. God assessed things and instantly realized something very special...something very intimate...was still lacking.

"And the Lord God said, It is not good that the man should be alone; I will make him an help meet for him." (Genesis 2:18).

So, God tested a few things to see if any would fill the void He saw in Adam. This premise reflects the artistic genius within God's creative process. He started by literally creating "every beast of the field, and fowl of the air" (Gen. 2:19) and introducing them to Adam. Now, when you really think about it, that's a lot of doing!

I associate the idea of "every beast of the field...and fowl of the air" with people we experience within the process of dating, or in our individual quest for "The One." We may not consciously recognize our actual yearning. But most of us sense a void within ourselves. What God saw was that there was only one unique piece, or "The One", capable of perfecting His greatest work in Adam. So, he extracted a vital part of Adam and formed something, or rather someone, even greater. He perfected Adam through Eve. But let's not get ahead of ourselves. We'll get more into this later. For now, let's take "getting naked" a step further.

Being "naked" means more than simply having the desire to reveal everything to that special, God-appointed mate for you. The fact is there is an unyielding and indescribable energy (or spirit) emanating out of your connection representing the true beauty between the two of you that suddenly empowers and compels you to expose all of yourself to your true husband or wife. It's a feeling that gives you unprecedented confidence in the other individual. Suddenly, there is a "need" to trust in a new and greater realm of existence and possibility that is exclusive to the two of you. Complete and unadulterated honesty becomes a requirement. This feeling is unlike anything you have ever experienced and it's open to all aspects of your life. It's as if anything less would be uncivilized.

But here's the thing: That "nakedness" described also represents a degree of "freedom" unlike anything you have ever experienced. It is this "freedom" that establishes a "peace which passeth all understanding" (Phil. 4:7). Why? That's simple. Having this freedom affords the two of you the ability to love each other fearlessly and with your whole heart. It elevates you to a place where you can transform and experience everything God made you to be for yourself and for each other…to be "naked and unashamed."

One of the most notable facets of the "perfect love" is your innate ability to suddenly recognize "The One" God created to complete you. This is often revealed long before the nuptials and applying for the wedding license. When you connect with "the One", you will discover a compulsion to share things with each other that you never desired to share with anyone previously. You suddenly have an unction to become intimately familiar with everything that constitutes your husband or wife-to-be. More than that, you somehow have the capacity to accept him or her and everything that makes them who they are even where this would otherwise be unacceptable or unimaginable.

I have had my share of ups and downs. There are things that I am extremely proud of and there are things I would prefer to imagine never took place, let alone share or discuss. And for most of my life, as in the case of Adam, I was okay with this. There are just things that many of us would rather exclude when sharing our backstories. But then…. When you happen to cross paths with "the One", suddenly there is a need to have nothing hidden or secret between the two of you. You begin to realize that secrets, undisclosed information, and lies would impede this amazing and new existence. You suddenly crave to experience a degree of life never-before-recognized. You want to live the God life. For the first time, there is a need to be completely "naked and unashamed." Suddenly, you want him or her to know everything about you. And they, in turn, want to become acquainted with the most intimate and secret parts of you. This is not another hook-up or everyday dating experience. This is "the One" who God created to complete you.

"…but all things are naked and open unto the eyes of Him with whom we have to do." Hebrews 4:13.

The entire premise behind "getting naked and being unashamed" is that it affords a husband and a wife the opportunity to be reborn into one singular creation. When the secrets are eliminated; when the worst has been revealed and accepted; and when you each accept, agree, and begin to truly appreciate the gift that God has given the two of you in each other, you are able to love each other unconditionally and at a level that will appear to be impossible to most of the world. Your lives have been perfected through a love asserted by God.

This type of love establishes an environment where there is no question that your spouse can't ask and no information that you are not comfortable sharing. In fact, the only individuals possessing the authority to disturb a union established by God is the husband and the wife. That's it! That is why the Word states "no man can put asunder" (Matt. 19:6). When God creates a bond, it's everlasting unless the husband or the wife under the covenant forsakes it. But even that does not mean the bond is permanently destroyed or irreparable.

Now, this may be difficult to accept based on your own prior experience. But within the "perfect love", the mistakes of a husband or a wife do not necessarily negate what God ordained before the two of you ever graced the earth. In fact, a union that God has put together is much greater and stronger than the man and woman under this covenant may realize. Remember, a husband and a wife within a "perfect love" are intended to make God's most perfect work demonstrable. That man or woman have each experienced their own version of trying various "beasts" and "fowls" in their individual quest for the "perfect love." Most of us have been there. But there's something about tapping into a vein of existence that is on par with what God has set apart for just the two of you that is uniquely distinguishable from every other previous experience or individual. When you align yourself with someone God created for you, you begin to identity a life that is more than anything you could have ever conceived independently. This is because the perfect love requires God.

That spirit empowering you with the unmitigated confidence and earnest "need" to expose all of yourself to each other extends light years beyond merely having the open-mindedness to accept all that constitutes your covenant partner. Within a perfect love, you are elevated to a place where somehow the issues, fears, and imperfections "the one" may be concerned with are not simply overlooked. The very thought of that very special man or woman, including those beautiful issues and imperfections, makes their unique individualism that much more adored.

But here's the rub outside of God: Most of us will never be that open and honest with most people. Typically, we are not okay with the idea of exposing that much of ourselves to most of the people we will ever meet. Sure. We may offer bits and pieces of ourselves for the sake of appearances and in the process of initiating or preserving a relationship. But in most instances, even the closest of relationships have certain, often profoundly intimate, and extremely personal parts of their life that will always remain off-limits. Many will go as far as leading others to believe that they have exposed all of themselves and lovingly accept every part of the other regardless of how disturbing those parts may actually be. Unfortunately, most of the time and with most people, this is generally a courteous misrepresentation of how they truly feel or over-expectation.

Again, we are not going to share everything in an everyday set of circumstances. We're too worried about the ramifications or fall-out of that type of decision. What will she say? What will he think? Likewise, most are not as open to seeing and hearing everything about most other people. The truth is that, apart from "the one" God has created and designated as your partner within the "perfect love," certain parts will always remain "covered" because we are typically too "ashamed" or afraid of a negative outcome or reaction.

Using Adam and Eve again as an example, these two were like teenagers at the inception of their union. They were "innocent" in the truest sense of the expression, which made their love pure and unvarnished. Their union had been created and divined by God Himself. Eve was, quite literally, a part of Adam, and Adam appreciated this very distinctive and visceral quality in Eve. They both knew each other as profoundly as they knew themselves. They were in "paradise" not simply because they lived in the Garden of Eden. Their "paradise" was based on the fact there was nothing between them that could disturb what God had established. Adam's appreciation for Eve was boundless because she was an extension of himself.

"Husbands should love and value their wives as they do their

own bodies. When a husband cares about his wife, he's actually caring about himself because the two of them are one." Ephesians 5:28 (Clear Word Translation).

Adam and Eve were God's own illustration of what it is like to "get naked" and to be "unashamed" in light of His perfect work and love in them.

You see, the perfect love introduces a certain innocence and "acceptable vulnerability" that the man and the woman often aspired but never truly and consistently achieved until connected to "the One." Why? Because "the One" personifies the full manifestation of God's greatest life experience for our lives. The "One" represents that single missing piece to completing the puzzle of life and love. "The One" is your perfection. Separate, the man or that special woman may be flawed. But together, there are none like the two of you, or what your combined love symbolizes, which is ultimately the Creator.

"The name of the Lord is a strong tower: the righteous runneth into it, and is safe." Proverbs 18:20.

"Getting naked and being unashamed" reflects the safety and strength that is innate in God's chosen husband and wife; one that "no man can put asunder." A man will know his wife is "the One" long before they finally succumb to what God has shown them, and before informally or spiritually committing themselves to each other. For example, I met a guy who found a woman who was instantly endowed with the unmitigated unction to marry him the very first day they met. Strangely, he had the same compulsion. Now, she never said anything seriously about it, and neither did he. So, they elected to go into a direction that they thought, or hoped, might be the most practical or prudent path to take even though their hearts were leading them into a very different direction. The result was that he consequently deferred what God had intended for more than a decade.

I remember him describing how it was when they would occasionally go to lunch in the beginning. The woman would often joke and say, "We should just go and get married." In response, he would often jokingly remark, "Well, let's go!" They never allowed themselves to actually go for what God had shown was the perfect path. So, eventually, they stepped away and began living separate lives. A few years later, they each found themselves in situations that were, let's just say, a little less than "perfect." He was involved with someone who he knew was not what God intended. Likewise, she had done the same. As a result, they both lost precious time that God always intended for them to spend together.

Now, the overtly "religious" might attempt to suggest, perhaps it wasn't God's perfect time for the two of them. And perhaps in any other instance, they may have been right except for one simple reason: They each knew better. They both realized that it was due to their own selfish attempts at creating their own solution versus choosing the path God had shown that their time together was impeded. Consider this:

"And I have also established my covenant with them, to give them the land of Canaan, the land of their pilgrimage, wherein they were strangers." Exodus 6:4.

God promised and set aside exclusively for His chosen people - the Israelites - a land that they would be able to occupy and claim as their own. It was a beautiful, fertile place. But it never should have taken 40 years to reach that Promised Land. In fact, the ONLY reason that their arrival was delayed was due to their own disobedience and perpetual unwillingness to comply with God's instructions. He promised the land to them. And if you believe what the songwriter says, "What God has for me is always for me." But they were too distracted.

Meanwhile, God continued to want the absolute best for His people. All that He needed them to do was to respect and follow His instructions. Yet, they were unwilling. They continuously chose to attempt to create their own alternative. This regarded not only the Promised Land, but God Himself. Now, maybe this is just me, but THAT'S insane! But still, God continued to "hope" that they would allow Him to give them what He always intended.

You see, God did not set out to block them from receiving

the gift He desired for them to have. What would be the point? The real issue was not about God's timing but their obedience. The challenge was that they repeatedly set out to get there by choosing their own path. But if they would have simply chosen the path that God had given, the generation that consequently never made it inside of the Promised Land would have been there to experience the gift that He had given. Denial was never God's aim. If that would have been the case, their children would have never occupied the land.

Now, I realize that Moses and the choices of the Israelites may be a little extreme. But this story also illustrates how we have a tendency of blaming God when He apparently has a much greater, immediate gift waiting to place into our immediate lives. Yes! He does things in His own time. But contrary to what many of the "uber-religious" would like for you to believe, His timing is not always years AFTER what we hoped or desired. In more cases than not, He desires for us to receive it now, or when we are actually ready or responsible enough to manage it. The challenge is our "readiness" is often suspect. As a result, God's timing is often thrown off by our own doing.

There are many stories in the Word that are demonstrable of this type of human error. I believe that many of today's stories regarding matters of the heart have a tendency of leading back to what "we" feel is best. Our focus turns towards figuring out how quickly "we" can satisfy our immediate desires instead of worrying about God's plan. We often turn our backs on God's vision for what's best for our lives.

Perhaps you are with the love that God intended but you have neglected to let everything go. The thought of extending everything to another person can be scary. Perhaps you're afraid of being let down or disappointed...again. In fact, there are probably a host of "perhaps" that could be proposed. For many of us, we are taught from childhood that there are certain things that simply should not be discussed, especially for women. Society has created this anathema by affixing labels and attaching us to certain conduct that seems best until we regret. So, we attempt to hide everything and everyone from our pasts. The result is years of frustration. No one wants to spend decades of their life worrying about some embarrassing little secret coming out. But then there's "The One" within the "perfect love." Imagine having a life with absolutely nothing between the two of you.

If you are experiencing these fears with your life, I encourage you to go to Jesus in prayer. He will give you the confidence to let go so that you can begin living in His perfect love, "naked and unashamed."

It's not too late to start today. Maybe you can take a weekend, just you and your wife or husband, to spend that time together opening up. Now, if you invite her or him into this newness of life, realize that honesty can be a rough pill to swallow. In other words, everything you hear may not be music to your ears at first. But with the right heart and spiritual connection, it will be a healing balm. At the end of the day, it's not about attempting to confirm what you may have always suspected adversely or uncovering reasons to throw the blame from you to him or her. It's about giving you both the opportunity to live and enjoy life and love in a way God always intended. In a manner of speaking, it's about letting go, and giving God the authority to do what He does naturally, or supernaturally, when you are engaged or married.

But a question that you may still have is: How will I know that he or she is "The One" that I can honestly trust and allow myself to "get completely naked and to be unashamed?" Or even more fundamentally, what is it to be "The One?" If this is your question, then we're already beginning to head into the right direction.

CHAPTER THREE
HOW TO IDENTIFY "THE ONE"

N. D. "Indy" Brennan

How To Identify "The One"

"...this is a companion to make man complete. She is my flesh and bone; she's like me, and she will be known as woman because she came out of me...The two of them shall become one person." Genesis 2:23-24 (Clear Word).

This is probably one of the most exciting topics within this book to me. "Identifying the One" unveils the severe disparity between fantasies of man and the realities of God. In fact, when the "One" comes into fruition, his or her existence rejects the worldly viewpoint that this person is nothing more than a romantic figment of one's imagination. Many people do not believe this type of perfectness can be experienced in "real life," because most can never imagine the existence a "perfect love" either. But there again lies the difference between God's loving perfection and the world's objection.

The irony in the world's attempt to deny the possibility of "The One" are those individuals who are willing to make themselves vulnerable. These are people who, despite past pains, look forward to sharing all of themselves to the "right" person. And if they are willing to share all of themselves to someone else, how can there be others who won't give as much to them.

"The One" is not merely a dream or fantasy or delusion of some sort. She or he will "seem" like a dream come true. That much is accurate. But that's the beautiful part of God's plan. She is literally HIS dream for you come true. Can you imagine that? God's dream come true for you?

But that's also why the feeling of "astonishment" is inescapable. Once you experience that one person who embodies the profound magnitude of God's love for you, people tend to become a little awestruck. But it is this experience that galvanizes admiration, adoration, appreciation, and love.

The fact is that you'll find that you simply cannot help yourself, regardless of whether you are the man or the woman in the covenant. It's a feeling that defies all concepts of worldly logic or reasoning. Understand that others who may never have experienced the "perfect love" may not be willing to accept your reality. But within you... You will discover that everything that he or she, or the two of them together, connect with will be filled with a warmth equivalent to sitting on the sun.

"But my dove, my perfect one, is unique." Song of Solomon 6:9 (NIV).

"The One" is described as a person possessing such an unfathomable, holy, distinct, and quintessential position in your life that, despite her "worldly" considered shortcomings, the Word defines her as being "undefiled" (Song of Solomon 6:9 KJV), meaning "untainted, uncorrupted, or pure." I want you to consider this for a moment...

Women, I want you to consider the fact that according to the Word of God, you are much more valuable, of much greater worth, meaning, and necessity than whatever your past or even your present actions, thoughts, and circumstances might suggest. The fact is that your very existence holds a divine purpose, and it is within that purpose that, through the grace of God, you are made "undefiled." In other words, His grace and purpose in and for your life makes you the pinnacle of virtuous perfection for that one, unique man. THAT can NEVER be taken away from you or physically removed. Meditate on that.

You see, you are so immensely special that you instill perfection in that man's otherwise broken or incomplete life. God created you for the primary purpose of completing His work in the man, the husband. Without you, he's only a fraction of himself. He can only see, understand, and even experience only so much life. But in you...because of you...and through his connection to you...in fact, just in merely finding you...he is suddenly enlightened to all of God's potential in and for his life, and the lives of his family.

I need you to realize that is how infinitely affective and

special you are, not only to that man but, most importantly to God Himself.

There are so many relationships that are unfortunately impeded because the woman has been made to feel or has independently settled on the false worldly perception that she is unworthy, decadent, or defiled. So, when she finally connects with her "One," she tends to self-destruct, unconsciously undermining God's actual intent for his and her life due to her derogated self-worth.

Ladies, I need you to understand that your perfection or perfectness is not contingent on what the world may think or even how you lived your life yesterday. In fact, outside of that union or separated from the "whole," you may have gone through or even done some things that you have lived to regret; or made decisions that you wish you could change today. It's called being human. But here's something that I hope that by reading this you will come to understand: Your very existence constitutes the key to perfection in the "one" God very purposely created and designated just for you. Despite what others may say or think, regardless of what may have occurred in the past, I encourage you never to forget that within you is unadulterated and absolute perfection. You are God's perfection - undefiled and wonderful.

Within him, whether he is cognizant of it or not, that man lacks a vital part of himself. He's literally incomplete or broken. But in the beauty and absolute genius behind God's design, that one woman or "wife," actual or betrothed, has been essentially created primarily to bring wholeness, completion, balance, and perfection to the entire life force of that "one" particular, unique man. The beauty of the love that God has for the two of you (and I really hope that you can fully appreciate the magnitude of what I am about to say) is that, together, through the grace of God, you are forged into a singular, new "creation" in Christ.

"Therefore, if anyone be in Christ, he is a new creation" (NIV); *"old things are passed away; behold all things are become new."* (KJV) 2 Corinthians 5:17.

This is a vital point that I want to make certain you understand. Genesis 2:24 (NIV) explains that when that man unites with "The One", the two become "one flesh." In other words, regardless of your past, when you are joined with God's chosen "One" for your life, the two of you are transformed into a single, new, and perfect individual, and past is gone forever. It is that man's responsibility to appreciate this newness, and your responsibility to assert it. That's the hard part, not as much for him as it is, so often, for the woman or the "wife."

What the Word tells us is that you are no longer bound to that past. At the very moment that the two of you connect or are bound together in the Spirit, you are instantly "undefiled" and pure, and now equipped to conceive a pure and "perfect love" with The One that God has timelessly conjugated with you. United, you are a new creation. Old things, again, are passed away, gone, eradicated. All that you have to do is find the confidence to "let yesterday go."

I felt it necessary to dedicate a few moments to helping women understand the real equity of her purpose and existence.

"And the Lord God said, It is not good that man should be alone, I will make him an help meet for him. And out of the ground the Lord God formed every beast of the field and every fowl of the air; and brought them unto Adam to see what he would call them...but for Adam there was not found any help meet for him." Genesis 2:18-20.

For years I read this scripture and envisioned simply what was literally described in the passage: God created all these animals, and eventually got around to creating Eve. But while praying and studying for this section, I grew to understand something very important: "The One" is unlike any other being in this universe. Let me explain.

Every man who has ever gone through the dating process can attest to the fact that he has probably gone through his fair share of "beast in the field" and "fowls of the air." Consider the various relationships that we go through along the path of attempting to find "The One." In most cases, we are not even aware that this is what we are searching for. Ironically, if we never experienced this "diverse" group within our search, we possibly would not be to appreciate the "One" when brought into our lives.

You may still ask: What makes ME so "wonderful?" Well, let's begin with this: "Wonder" is defined as "a person...causing astonishment and admiration; a marvel; or the feeling aroused by something strange, unexpected, etc."

Adam had a virtual cornucopia of options to choose from. But none of them rose to the level that God envisioned to complete his life. Adam on the other hand, in his own limited thinking, was probably fine with what he had. He did not know that something greater even existed. Remember without Eve, his perception was based primarily on his limited understanding and experience. So perhaps for Adam, having lions, tigers, and bears to accompany him seemed, at least at the time, sufficient. But God saw something much greater in what He was building in him.

When a woman connects with a "man" within the "perfect love," you both experience something that resembles the "feeling aroused by something strange [and] unexpected." The mere presence or essence of the "One" is a marvel, causing unrealized "astonishment and admiration." And while any other man, apart from God's intended, may believe he is the one who is special, the "One" recognizes his suddenly amazing life is based on you.

"Whoever findeth a wife findeth a good thing, and obtaineth favour of the Lord." Proverbs 18:22.

"Favour" means that you are suddenly in the V.I.P. lane with God. It means that a man is suddenly elevated to a greater level of understanding, empowerment, and existence. When he is in covenant with that one special woman, he is instantly raised to a higher level of spiritual enlightenment. That is how awesome you are! God designed you with such unimaginable significance that the Book of Proverbs (4:9) refers to you as the man's "ornament of grace" and his "crown of glory.' Allow me to make this even a little clearer for you.

The verse reads, "Whoever findeth a wife findeth a good thing." Very few people apprehend the magnitude of this promise. That's right! I said a "promise."

"The Word defines the "wife," or the "One," as a "good thing." There are those who believe that if you study the etymology of the word "good," you would discover that the word "good" derives from the word "God." So, if finding a wife is a "good thing," then what the Word is actually telling us is when a man finds "The One," his "wife," he has essentially found a "God thing"...or patent evidence of God's literal existence. Your new covenant life symbolizes the fulfillment of God's promise.

"Every good gift and every perfect gift is from above, and cometh down from the Father of lights." James 1:17.

I want you to understand something: Ladies, you are not just another "gift" from God. No. The fact is that you embody the greatest gift that God has ever given to man. In fact, being much more specific, to that one man, or your "One," in particular. And men, I need you to understand and appreciate that the "One" is resounding evidence of how fortunate you are and how much more exceptional your life has become due to your connection to the "One."

In the context of the Word of God, "The One" - meaning the wife - comes from God Himself. And when you finally realize what God has given you in the "One," the thought of ever hurting her, the thought of ever cheating on her, the very idea of failing to honor her existence is suddenly absurd. The "One" represents the physical evidence of God's favor over your life. Suddenly arguments begin to become inconsequential except in the context of building the two of you up. In your eyes, there is no woman that is more beautiful, enchanting, alluring, adorable, or sensual than your "One".

It sort of just happens. The traditional womanizer suddenly loses his taste for anyone outside of the "One." The man in doubt is suddenly transported to a place where, when it comes to "The

N. D. "Indy" Brennan

One," there is no longer a question or worry. That guy who was working to refrain from letting everything go suddenly discerns the senselessness of it all. He acquiesces to God's presence in her. He submits to her brilliance and power. But...it isn't as if he gains nothing in the process, as some with a more "worldly" perspective may attempt to suggest. No. Suddenly, every part of his life just seems right or better even though the situation or physical circumstances may appear to be the same. Food tastes differently. You sleep more restfully. You inherit the confidence to love her wholly and completely. Life just feels...well...great! Or, just maybe...dare I say...as "God intended. Why? Because you are favored by God, and, I don't know about you, but being favored or preferred by God is so much better than ANY alternative.

You may have rough days. There may be times when you may not know how you will make it or how you will deal with whatever you may be facing. And then suddenly...something as speciously insignificant, as miniscule, or as simple as a text from her sent strangely at just the right time; or just hearing her say "Heyyyyy!!' excitedly when you may have called for no specific reason; or maybe...just maybe...just the thought of her...and suddenly, in an instant, everything is somehow, unexplainably, as right as rain...perfect. How? The answer becomes as obvious to you as it is mystifying to others outside of your covenant: It's God.

When you come to understand the gift that has been withheld from you and then, unexpectedly, placed into your life through her, you subtly begin to appreciate life, real life, as God truly intended. She lights the pathway of your otherwise dimmer world view.

Now, you may be saying, "What?! I don't have a dim world view!" Well, here's the thing: You only know or believe what you can see or what you have been able to envision alone - meaning before or without "The One." So, much as the earlier example of Adam when he was alone in the Garden of Eden and before God created Eve, it is no surprise that you may naturally adopt this belief. But I challenge you to imagine a life that exceeds your own imagination...a life that is greater than anything you could ever cogently experience without "The One." Imagine merely the possibility of things being even more awesome, by leaps and bounds, than it may even seem today...a life that you cannot necessarily envisage but that is still attainable...somehow. That possibility, that hope, that inkling of even a chance of experiencing something higher or greater...that's what you will discover in "The One" that God has for your life. Sure, you may not be able to measure it in gold, but what is gold anyway when compared to a perfect life, the perfect love, and actually finding the "One?"

Remember that the key to life and living, real living, is her, "The One" - the wife. But likewise, for every woman, remember also that there is that "one" particular, divine man or husband. It's funny. While men have challenges accepting the reality of "The One," women have often complicated God's intent as well.

A woman once spoke with me about a book she personally

believed could assist in preventing others from missing what God had designed for their life through this enchanted connection. The theme stemmed from an expression or idea that most of us are often intimately acquainted with. It's about when you get sick and tired of being sick and tired, AND you fully commit to doing things God's way...When you FINALLY say, "No more Ishmaels!"

CHAPTER FOUR
NO MORE ISHMAELS!

No More Ishmaels!

"My plan is to make a great nation from your descendants, a different people, and I will bless you, and through you all nations of the earth will be blessed...my intention is for you to be a blessing to the whole world." Genesis 12:2-3 (Clear Word).

"Ishmaels" are the results of when we steer away from what we know God has promised to us in the "One." "Ishmaels" are those men or women, and yes, even those husbands or wives, that WE choose instead of waiting for what He has designated for us. "Ishmaels" are often what we have before, outside of, or until we find the "One." But I guess the biggest thing is that "Ishmaels" are often "life" decisions made separate from God. But here's what's interesting: Sometimes we must experience the "Ishmaels" in order to understand and to appreciate it when "Isaac" is born into our lives. Let me explain.

"Which forsaketh the guide of her youth, and forgeteth the covenant of her God." Proverbs 2:17.

Men are known for screwing up. Even though statistically the two practically parity one another, men are often looked upon as

47

the one who typically takes advantage of his "one," forgetting about those special holidays, birthdays, and whatever other days that have been designated, often by you, as days that "should" be honored and remembered. If you were to look up the definition of "infidelity," there's a pretty good chance that you will find the picture of "some" guy next to the word, or at least that is the depiction that society has led us to believe, even if merely in jest. It is the man that is almost expected, if it happens within a union, to neglect to apprehend the wonder and infinite brilliance that his "One" embodies in her very existence.

Okay, I get it! And let's be honest, many guys do fall within this category. But women...you may be much more subtle and traditionally assigned less culpability for corrupting what would otherwise be the "Perfect Love." But women have also been known to fall short of the mark, becoming distracted, and, once actually finding "The One," treating him with the same regard as you may have done with some of your former "beasts" and "fowls," or worse.

Allow me to remind women as well that there ARE those men who remember every holiday and any day that happens to be remotely special to you. In fact, there are those who are independently inspired to create or acknowledge special days, even outside of those you may recognize in honor of you or something that the two of you may have accomplished or experienced together.

But there are also those that may not always remember to place the seat down in the bathroom, or remember every holiday, or always say the right things. Does that mean that he is not "The

One?" Well, that's a question you must ask yourself, and one that we will be digging deeper into when we get into "Understanding Your Love Requirements" because each one of us, male and female, have very distinct needs - things that we require. These are things that we simply cannot acquiesce within the type of loving relationship that will best service each one of us individually, and that will ultimately make us whole.

But much as in the case of the man when he finds the "One," I would like to encourage you to consider that the "One" actually works both ways. God has set aside, exclusively just for you, that one individual who literally exists to fulfill every need and desire that you have, regardless of how seemingly insignificant. Remember that as He created you to perfect that man, the "One" is there to also perfect you. It is the two of you together, conjugated in God's perfectness within "the perfect love," that inevitably forms your oneness, and that makes your being whole.

Through the "One," you are instantly made perfect, undefiled, and even more wonderful than you were before or without "The One." He allows you to enter his life and transform it into what God had already preordained the two of you to become. It's special. It's unique.

But it's like that only with the "One" for and with you. But that's also the part that you must not forget. When you connect to "The One," yesterday is gone! Regardless of what may have previously discouraged you, embarrassed you, or things that you

N. D. "Indy" Brennan

feared others would discover about you, a substantive part of his role is to ensure that you never forget how wonderful you truly are and the insatiable influence that you hold over his life.

The challenge is that women are often just as guilty of corrupting what God has put together as men. You are fortunate enough to have been endowed and empowered with "The One," but then you allow your past proclivities, habits, weaknesses, fears, or influences to invade the perfectness that God is establishing within the two of you. As I will continue to remind you, "what God has put together no man [or woman for that matter] can put asunder." In other words, only you or your husband or wife has the power to allow anyone or anything to taint what the two of you have together, that perfect love in Christ. So, here's a bit of simple advice: When you are finally joined to The One - that one man that you KNOW within EVERYTHING in you is God's personal and perfect gift to you; who He has shown you has been created especially for you; and who is essentially intended to be your everything - don't mess it up. Trust me. There is nothing, and I mean NOTHING, that is greater than what God has given. Anything outside of His promise is...well...your own personal "Ishmael."

"God is not a man that He should lie; neither the son of man, that He should repent: hath He said, and shall He not do it? Or hath He spoken, and shall not make it good?" (Numbers 23:19). The

answer is simply "*no.*" "*Thy word is true from the beginning.*" (Psalms 119:160).

The word "promise" often holds unrealized potential, potential that most of us, sadly enough, do not have the patience and persistence to realize in the process of manifestation. Many people blame it on technology and the fact that, today, we want everything now. But if you were to go back to, for example, the exodus of Moses and the people of Israel from Egypt, their collective downfall was their anxiety. They wanted God's promise fulfilled NOW too, therein failing to realize that the very fact they had been freed from bondage and had been given the authority to walk of their own volition into the "promised land," the "promise" had already been fulfilled.

You see, using this as the example again, the land was already there. They just couldn't keep their hearts and minds stayed on it. The "promise" was there, but they failed to realize it due to the worldly or more common perspective of their immediate circumstances. The question I ask is: How many times can you remember falling subject to the same type of individually-inspired spiritual abjection or shut down in faith? How many times have you realized, after the fact, that you had, indeed, turned your focus away from the promise or found yourself distracted?

The reason that I chose to use the above-referenced scripture is that, regardless of it being a promise made by a man, by a woman, or by God Himself, the equity of that promise rests in the faith that you have and continue to maintain in its author to do what he, she or God said they would do.

People may disappoint you. They may make so-called "promises" that seem to never come to fruition. Don't get me wrong. Their hearts may be in the right place. But they were simply unable to or incapable of accomplishing whatever it was that they "promised" would be done. And yes, there are some who are simply liars, having no actual and sincere intent to even do half of what they had unmitigatedly assured you would be done or taken care of for that matter. But, again, there's God. There has never been a promise documented that He has ever failed to deliver, especially where the recipient of that promise held up to his or her end of the deal. He is not a man that He should lie because His Word is always true. If He said it, it will come to past. If He promised it, you can rest assured that He will make good on His word. He has proven this repeatedly, as consummately demonstrated when it came to the earthly life, death, and resurrection of His own Son.

"She is my flesh and bone; she's like me, and she will be known as woman because she came out of m[e]...the two of them shall become as one person." Genesis 2:23-24 (Clear Word).

There are certain couples that even for those that may not completely buy into the concept, let alone believe in the possibility of a "perfect love," that would yet concede to the fact that on some unknown or ethereal level, "These two were made for each other." It's where they are not simply compatible. They are unquestionably, almost annoyingly, the "Ken and Barbie" of the human product line. I'm talking about a man and a woman of varying personalities that are almost bizarrely, unequivocally perfect for each other. It's like the thought of either individual deciding one day to suddenly break away from the other would be...well...laughable; that apparent perfectness where even the mere suggestion of one leaving the other is instantly detracted to somewhere along the lines of "You've got to be kidding me!"

These often seemingly unremarkable individuals constitute the fortunate few that God deems it appropriate, or necessary, to convene or bring together while everyone else stands around mystified, and cynically asking, "What about me?!" It's where their love for each other is as immediate and as innate, often from the very start, as a baby inhaling and exhaling for the very first time.

When I was in my early twenties there was a couple, distant family members, who fell within, at least at the time, this nauseatingly, exhaustingly amorous group. In all honesty, they had a marriage to die for.

Contrary to today's ridiculous standards, he wasn't some industry-leading, media mogul, a marquee athlete, or a prominent entertainer selling out arenas. Likewise, she was nowhere near the dystrophic, media-hoarding, feminine megalomaniacs that we have become so accustomed to watching on "reality" television today. In fact, gauging them by today's standards, they should have been miserable, when, in reality, they lived quite remarkably to the contrary.

The husband was a 6'2" industrial worker. His wife, well, as far back as I can recall, spent much of her time working as a full-time homemaker and helping to raise their 2 children. Both had amazing personalities, not necessarily "wealthy," but, still, lived in a fairly nice community within the town that they were residing. And as if to drive the nail home a little further, they were a rather attractive couple. In reality, considering the state of my life at the time, I not only admired them, I was actually quite fond of them. I often, quietly, longed for what they had achieved. It was one of "those" types of marriages - The ones that you hate to admit you envy, but still...you really envy. Anyone with half of a brain and a sliver of a heart could see that they had been literally created for each other. This was only God's doing. So, the obvious question is: What on earth could go wrong in this situation? God had given them, seemingly, everything - the perfect love. He had fulfilled His promise by giving the two of them together, a life that breathed with every living, waking breath "peace and wholeness."

"The thief cometh not, but for to steal, and to kill, and to destroy: I am come that they might have life, and that they might have it more abundantly." John 10:10.

The wife began to speak with other people and question her significance at home. The husband, being a good and supportive husband - you know, that guy who is ALWAYS encouraging you, who believes in you unrelentingly, and who ONLY wants to do whatever makes YOU happy because YOUR happiness defines his happiness - well, she began venturing out looking for "something" that would bring more significance and meaning to her life. This is emblematic of the story of the children of Israel, Sarah, and Abraham, and so many other stories like it.

Now, allow me to digress momentarily. I am in no way attempting to suggest by any stretch of the imagination that a woman should not strive to work, or start her own business, or feel great in being a homemaker. Again, every one of us is different. Our needs, individually and as one conjoined unit, are distinct to each one of our own designations. In fact, it is those characteristics that helps to round out their lives.

One thing that we need to always take into consideration, especially when soliciting the opinion of others, is that the two of you are special, unique, and set apart from anyone else. You are two unique individuals that have been literally created just for each other. Recognize and work not to depreciate that very distinguishable interest the two of you, alone, have in each other. Always remember what He has for you, or the two of you, is specially made for the two of you.

Appreciate who He has made you, especially in, your oneness. Don't devalue the awesome power, energy, and impact that He has entrusted in you just for the purpose of perfecting your very special bond. It is often these distractions, let alone unexpected and often dire circumstances, that tend to introduce "Ishmael-like" opportunities, apart from God. Remember, the greatest gift God has given to you is each other. Therefore, respect God's presence.

"She said to Abram, 'The Lord has still not given us a child but maybe we could have one through Hagar and begin our family that way. Why don't you sleep with her.'" Genesis 16:2 (Clear Word).

At the time, multi-level marketing was a rage. Companies such as Herbalife, ACN, and a host of others had begun popping up everywhere. The meetings were motivational and inspiring. She began feeling that, perhaps, this was her "calling."

She soon started working with the organization under an older man who was the polar opposite of her husband physically and emotionally. But he encouraged her in ways she had never previously experienced. She began seeing things in him that, this new "spirit," led her to believe that her husband could not match. She became an instant success within the organization under the close tutelage of her new mentor. What she did not apprehend until she was far too gone was that this "mentor" had an underlying motivation. He was subtly coming for her.

"Nevertheless, let every one of you in particular so love his wife even as himself; and the wife see that she reverences her husband." Ephesians 5:33.

She began to look upon her own husband as a lesser individual, at least compared to the mentor. And as the wife and the mentor continued to experience successes in business, their "closeness" grew, spawning thoughts that she had never had previously outside of her husband.

I believe that the seemingly impossible manifested itself during a business trip to a convention where the mentor and the wife travelled together to attend. Now, obviously, I wasn't in attendance at the meeting or there with the two of them. But somewhere along the way, this wife, and her mentor, both of which were married, began a purely sexual affair. I call it "purely" sexual, at least on the part of the mentor, because, as the wife shortly discovered, the mentor, as unhappy as he may have suggested with his home life, had absolutely no intention of separating from his wife.

This presents a question: Should one blame the mentor for manipulating the situation or the wife for choosing to entertain his advances or her sudden carnal desires? God had fulfilled a promise that she was about to break. This is what I call an "Ishmael," where we lose sight of or faith in what He has done or is doing in and for our lives. It is where we break or forfeit His promise.

I have always believed this: A woman or a man, a husband, or a wife, may be advanced upon by someone outside of their union. That can be considered a compliment. People may find you or your husband or wife attractive. That's not impossible. In fact, in some cases, it's quite likely. The glow flowing from a man and woman within a perfect union is often a magnet to the wrong element. As the passage reads in a separate translation, "thieves...are not interested in feeding the sheep, but rather feeding on them."

But it is also my belief that a "perfect love" "should" conquer all. The only person that can be blamed in a situation as described above is the covenant breaker.

The reality is, excluding the act of rape or being placed into some substance-induced stupor, the average individual is not going to "force" you to act on their advances. Likewise, a woman will never just fall on top of a naked man and a man will never just trip and fall inside of a naked woman, regardless of how "things just happen." This requires a conscious and irresponsible decision on your part. So, would I personally blame the mentor or the wife? Well, remember that only one or the two of you can corrupt the perfectness that God has created under your covenant.

Initially, the wife hid her affair from her husband but her actions in the house were grossly inconsistent with what her husband knew. But he - being that loving, trusting husband - chose to disregard this deviant spirit that had suddenly taken residence in their home.

She, in turn, became confused "emotionally," and finally told her husband, begging him to forgive her. The husband, traditionally docile in nature, was instantly crushed and angry. Their perfect bond had been chinked. Eventually, she began to realize what she had allowed to come into their lives. Her decision had given birth to an "Ishmael" when God had promised "Isaac."

But do you know what was so remarkable about the husband in the end? It was gut-wrenchingly obvious that he could never love any other woman. She was STILL his "one." That, believe it or not, despite the hurt and the complete annihilation of his immediate ability to trust her, incredibly did not change. Somehow, through Christ, he knew that he could not live without this woman. Somehow, through Christ, he would have to let things go and to find it in his heart to trust her again.

She had royally screwed up. There's no doubting that. And no one, not in this lifetime, could have blamed him if he would have left her and taken the children. But here was a man that truly and unrelentingly loved his wife, despite even what she had done. Was he hurt? Of course. They even separated for some time. In fact, it took almost a year to a year and a half for him to get to the point where he would not feel...see...or sense...the mark, the touch, the impression, left on his wife by another man. She pleaded for him, her husband in Christ, to rid them of this "Ishmael," and through this perfect love, he did.

You see, the mentor was her "Ishmael" - the result of a decision apart from God. Her husband was her "Isaac" - God's promise fulfilled. Sadly enough, even in her case, it took this "Ishmael" and the threat of losing all that God had established in her home to help her to truly understand the incalculable significance of her husband, and the life with her "Isaac."

"And all things are of God, who hath reconciled us to himself by Jesus Christ, and hath given us the ministry of reconciliation." 2 Corinthians 5:18.

I chose to share an experience that I was familiar with but also one that most people can appreciate. Even if you have been fortunate enough to have escaped the lure of infidelity, most of us are not, unfortunately, blind to the reality of this cancer that so often plagues relationships.

But here's the thing: "Ishmaels" are not limited to merely acts of sexual indiscretions outside of your union. Genesis 16:2 shows us where Sarai openly consented and actually encouraged Abram to solicit the outside assistance of her handmaiden Hagar for having a child, which the Word shows, once again, she later deeply regretted. It was actually Sarai's idea! In turn, Ishmael became a lifelong commitment that they, as a family, were forever bound. And that's the thing about many of the "Ishmaels" that we invite into our otherwise "perfect love." In many instances, it can take years to rise above our "Ishmaels." For some, it can extend for generations. But... It does not always have to be this way. The truth is that in a moment, in the blinking of an eye, just as Christ instantly forgives and accepts us back, we can and often find the courage to do the same for each other.

The "Ishmael" in most relationships tends to be that person outside of "The One." Having to wait on God can, at time, be rough. Having to trust and believe, unyieldingly, in His Word and His promise regarding "The One" can be trying. I'll give you that. Sarah waited practically for two and a half decades for the impossible to happen...for God's promise to be fulfilled and for Isaac to be born. That's not an easy task even for the best of us. I guess the point is that no one said it would be easy. But then again, the ease of it all goes back to your perspective - your ability to keep your eyes on the prize and continue to press towards the mark of His higher calling even when everything around you is screaming otherwise. Even when your flesh is craving otherwise. Even when it seems as if it will never happen from the world's perspective. But when you receive it...when you receive him or her...when "The One" finally enters your life...when "Isaac" is finally born...I assure you that the waiting will suddenly feel all worth the while.

Each one of us has to get to the point where we become so tired and in such need of who we KNOW He has created just for us that we come to the point where we consciously and very purposely deny all others and agree that we will no longer even entertain another "Ishmael." The aim evolves into: "I will not settle for anything less than Isaac!" No matter whom! No matter what! No matter how much time is required! Because within the "perfect love" rests more potential and possibilities and a type of reality that we cannot even begin to fathom. After years of being broken, how can we truly know what it is to be made whole? That can only be achieved through God...and His one for us.

It's in "Isaac" that we come to distinguish our needs from our wants - our love requirements. In fact, there are so-called "needs" that each one of us has that through Christ we discover are not even really all that important. "Isaac" fills those love requirements that we realize. But "Issacs" also satisfy needs we have yet to apprehend.

"Love requirements"...that divine ideology reaching into the deepest depths of your very being whose fulfillment makes everything...perfect. That's the promise...

What's yours? Let's see.

CHAPTER FIVE
UNDERSTANDING YOUR LOVE REQUIREMENTS

Understanding Your Love Requirements

"Every good and perfect gift is from above, coming down from the Father of heavenly lights." James 1:17. *"But each man has his own gift from God; one has this gift, another has that."* 1 Corinthians 7:7.

This is where every one of us, every couple or preordained union, is set apart from everyone else throughout the rest of the world, excluding "The One." It is because of this unprecedented uniqueness forming the two of you that perplexes others who may attempt to create a facsimile of what the two of you have together. But they can't. The "perfect love" is an unblemished and nonconforming type of love that is distinguishable only to the two people under this love. And when you really think about it, who has the power to improve a love that the Creator created perfectly? That's what also makes what the two of you have so obfuscating.

Think of it like this. That love connection - that "perfect love" that amalgamated the two of you together into one beautiful being - is unlike anyone else or any other couple in the universe. It's as indigenous to your spiritual make up as is your individual DNA. That's what makes it so incredibly special when you finally connect with "The One." I'm not simply attempting to describe your impossible-like love for each other for the sake of illustrating some literary fantastical imagery. The fact is that "fantastic" is exactly what this is: the physical manifestation of your most unbelievable fantasy for love multiplied times infinity. It is as nothing that could ever be accomplished purely of your own independent volition, except as ordained and inspired by God Himself. Nothing!

"Now I am precious to my husband. I am like a wall of solid gold with silver towers against the advances of others. In his love I have found contentment and peace...I also have a vineyard, and it's mine. But I have given it to you. I am now your vineyard; my darling, I am yours." Song of Solomon 8:10, 12 (Clear Word).

Your individual love requirements are as personal, as profound, and as intimate as those untold scents that, for some reason, quietly stimulate those special endorphins that ignite the senses and foments a seemingly unearthly yearning. It's like those special, subtle touches in just the right place at just the right time by just the right person...

You see, each one of us has unique and very individualized love requirements. These are those things that some of us are familiar with but many of which we are still learning we cannot achieve except within the "perfect love." In that these are unique qualities or needs He has placed inside of each one of us, God is quite aware of the needs that we require to be finally made whole. This is one of the primary purposes of "The One," whether referring to the husband or the wife.

As the scripture suggests, when you connect to "The One" within a "perfect love," her vineyard becomes, almost instinctively, your vineyard. Your life becomes her life.

In one of those awesome reflective moments, a woman once shared with her husband, "it absolutely amazes me that you love me the way that you do." Just to hear those words so sweetly and sincerely spoken warmed everything in him because he recognized that in that very special moment, she got it. She understood the unprecedented vastness, the breadth and depth, of not merely the insatiable love he had for her, but also the awesome love and power of God. He appreciated what his life had become through her. He adored every crack and crevice of this amazing woman who just happened to be his wonderful and perfect wife.

Others may hear the way that you describe your wife within the "perfect love" and feel that perhaps it's too much. One may think, "She may be a lot, but perfect?? Seriously?"

But his wife was unlike any other woman. In his eyes, she was an absolutely remarkable woman with seemingly infinite talents and a practically burdensome number of incredible ideas. To him, his wife possessed unquestionable, riveting, and breathtaking beauty. This woman had the audacity and boldness through her love for herself and Christ to love and accept him wholly and completely, and she loved him as eternally as he forever swore to love her. She, somehow, appreciated his imperfections, while giving him the courage to overcome his own unspoken insecurities. For him, his wife was perfect. She fulfilled every one of his needs, including those that he was unaware of until God brought her into his life. She is all these deliciously notable and distinguishable flavors and special seasonings that you just can't quite put your finger on; that spice of life that you never would have ordinarily considered but that turned out to be explosive and knee-bucklingly sensual just by grazing your palate. He often described her as that one special secret ingredient that forms that "oh-so perfect" dish.

But perfection is personal and subjective. It's a desire, a craving, or a yearning that places you and her or him, in a place that is isolated and intimate. It's a world where, suddenly, there is no one else that exists or no one that matters even remotely, except the two of you.

In many cases, we believe we know what we require for the "perfect love." We think to ourselves, "These are the things that I MUST have within my relationship" right? But honestly, you really will not truly understand until SHE or he happens, or God does what only He can do in your life. Remember, it's often that "spice" or "combination of spices" that YOU never would have even considered. What many fail to connect is that your love requirements are actually "life requirements" vital to your very existence. The "One" impacts more than you are capable of appreciating before being placed into your life.

"But exhort one another daily, while it is called Today; lest any of you be hardened through the deceitfulness of sin." Hebrews 3:13.

I've heard women comment, "He's going to HAVE to accept me for who I am." I've heard men say, "She's going to have to understand that it is what it is," whatever that means. But the mere fact that you feel the need to make these declarations identifies you as someone who is trying to disguise your fears and insecurities.

"Set your affections on things above, not on things on the earth." Colossians 3:2.

Love requirements are those, often, internal needs that you have where he somehow adores those things you have been afraid of exposing, or where she wants to work with you to build your impossible dream. It's where SHE occasionally belches at the table or where HE enjoys shopping. The thing is that everyone's love requirements are unique to that individual and, ultimately, to that union.

But love requirements are designed to give you peace and

security. They are intended to place you at such a level of comfort that you can be your real self; to bring you joy and to liberate you from those insecurities and inhibitions, at least when you are with "The One." Love requirements reveal a kinship and friendship, and a love that exceeds anything and anyone else imaginable. Love requirements are your personal breadcrumbs back into the Garden of Eden except its now located within your hometown.

That's why we should walk cautiously whenever attempting to advise others because every couple and their aggregate love requirements are distinct to their own independent union.

I had a woman tell me once, "If you loved me then you'd hit me!" Aside from the apparent "issues" she clearly had, it was obvious that I couldn't meet her love requirements. It wasn't me. It wasn't even her. It was us. I was not her "one," and vice-versa. Alternatively, you may have a man and a woman both enjoy playing basketball for example. So, they embrace any opportunity to play a loving game with each other. And if THAT gets a little "physical," in the best kind of way, then that's okay. The real joy comes as they uncover ways of working it out.

"You belong to the Lord and are set apart to be His very own. Out of all the people of the world, He has chosen you to be His treasured possession." Deuteronomy 14:2 (Clear Word).

THE PERFECT LOVE BOOK

The point is that your "one" is "The One" because somehow, almost magically, he or she is the key to life. The "One" somehow fits perfectly into every groove and every notch, or every rise and every fall, and somehow you do the same. The Word describes each one of us, meaning God's believers, as "a peculiar people." In the context of the scription, "peculiar" is not the same as being "weird," but rather a person or covenant that is special, holy, and set apart by God for a specific purpose. Each man has his own gift from God in his wife, separate, holy, and set apart. She embodies all that you require because she was made to be your key to life, just as you, the husband, are hers. She somehow meets, magnificently, all your love requirements.

Everything that you are and in everything that you do within the "perfect love" is suddenly inspired by the "One." Then one day, at the most unexpected time, she makes the most remarkable comment, "it absolutely amazes me that you love me the way that you do." You smile in response ingratiatingly and breathlessly and find yourself saying, "That's funny. I was just thinking the exact same thing about you."

There is nothing better than this...at least until entering into...

CHAPTER SIX
THE BED UNDEFILED

"The physical and emotional pleasures resulting from a faithful marriage relationship are ordained by God and held in honor of Him." (Standards of Sexual Morality, excerpt taken from The Full Life Study Bible referencing Hebrews 13:4).

N. D. "Indy" Brennan

The Bed Undefiled

"Wives, submit yourselves unto your own husbands, as unto the Lord...As the church is subject unto Christ, so let the wives be to their own husbands in everything. Husbands, love your wives even as Christ also loved the church, and gave himself for it; that he might sanctify and cleanse it with the washing of water by the Word...not having spot, or wrinkle, or any such thing; but that it should be holy and without blemish...For this cause shall a man be joined unto his wife, and they shall be one flesh. This is a great mystery." Ephesians 5:22-32.

The consummation of physical bodies between a man and woman - meaning a husband and his wife - within a "perfect love" should be unlike anything otherwise conceivable on this earth because it mirrors the power and passion, the sharing and the immense caring that is the cornerstone of the connection between the husband and the wife. A perfect love is encompassed by a perfect peace, and that perfect peace introduces a world of wonder, excitement, and unprecedented opportunity within the intimacy department, which is the greatest personal ministry within a marriage. The sexual relationship within a "perfect love" is an enigma simply because most fail to apprehend that this remarkable conjugation and cooperation reflects God's infinite and eternal love for us.

So, allow me to take a moment to explain what the church and our parents failed to teach with respect to the profound intimacy of the ministry of marriage...and in your "perfect love" with "The One."

"Blessed is the man that endureth temptation: for when he is tried he shall receive the crown of life, which the Lord hath promised that loved Him." James 1:2.

Many years ago, a close single, male friend of mine went out to a local club one night in Atlanta. My friend, in our younger years, was someone who was most typically referred to as a "hound," constantly sniffing around for something or someone that he "could get into." The truth is that he was one of the most noncommittal, relationship deferring individuals that I had ever met. Today, I understand that this was merely a facade to cloak his fear of being disappointed or, God forbid, being a disappointment to someone else that he really cared about. It's so amazing how this sensibility that was once a common tactic that primarily men used before the year 2000 to guard themselves from hurt or disappointment has crossed over into a common practice for many millennial women today.

While at the club he happened to meet a woman who he referred to years later as one of the most amazing women he had ever encountered. They danced, talked, and drank. And, eventually, as they say, "one thing led to another" and they found themselves transferred from inside of the club to his bachelor home. Later, he described this encounter as an experience that he never anticipated when he was preparing to go out, but a night that he would not soon forget.

It wasn't long before his female companion adopted a less subtle approach, evolving into this fearless, unusually assertive, and completely uninhibited woman that was suddenly 100% invested into this "moment" they were having. He admitted that she performed acts on him during this physical excursion that he had never experienced. She did things that made HIM turn "50 Shades of Grey."

Afterwards, exhausted and awestruck by what had just transpired, he assumed that she would be remaining for the evening. In his mind, they had something "magical," something that he thought was "special." An interesting point is that the more mature that we become, the more we understand matters of the heart. After years of "experimenting" myself, I've learned that in the eyes of man, at times, it can be hard to distinguish between the 3 "L's" - love, lust, and loneliness. (Now, there's a book title for you!) You see, while the latter two - lust and loneliness - had been a substantive part of their evening, the former - specifically "love" - was merely an illusion. He had simply been overwhelmed by the physical exchange that had occurred, and the fact that she had been so sexually unrestrained within their "intercourse" of events. But "love" was not what my friend, nor his companion, were experiencing.

Instead of staying for the evening, she politely yet abruptly began getting dressed and preparing to leave. This made what had just taken place that much more incredulous to my snubbed friend. He had applied this maneuver himself over the years and in several situations under various circumstances once the "deed" was done. But now, suddenly, his patented "move" was being performed against him. After everything that had taken place that evening, he could not understand how or why this was happening.

Desperately, he asked her if she could stay. She explained that, though it was a weekend night, she really had to get home to prepare for work. Again, this was a tactic that he had employed innumerably himself. For my friend, this didn't make any sense.

He asked her anxiously, practically pleading now, for a telephone number, suddenly realizing that he barely knew her name. Apprehensively, she gave him "a" telephone number and a quick obligatory kiss, now deeply regretting the evening's activities. She quietly exited and drove herself home, alone.

He called me the next morning anxious to share his amazing encounter, still fresh on his mind from just a few hours previous. He was one of those guys, as many of us toyed back then, that did not want to immediately call her. To some, that could come across as being overzealous or desperate. The fact is, he WAS desperate to speak with her again. He asked me, as if it really mattered, whether he should call. I, not that he required my blessing, gave him the go ahead just for him to soon discover that the "telephone number" she had given was, in fact, a pager. He became nervous because this was, again, a common ploy back in the late 80's and 90's for men and women who were really not interested or already involved in a relationship.

This woman had enchanted him with her complete lack of sexual reservations or inhibitions. He called several times to leave his number, desperately hoping to speak with her again. For days on end, his calls would not be returned. Sitting back and merely observing my friend, I slowly began to notice how his world was slowly diminishing. He began taking on these uncharacteristic and stalker-like proclivities for this woman who he had only known for a brief "moment." Here's the hard truth: He had become possessed by a spirit that he did not understand and he could not shake, and he wasn't trying to rid himself of it anytime soon. I, and many of our friends, did not understand what was happening at first. This was a purely carnal spirit that was seducing him on a level that was not noticeable to the unseasoned eye.

From what I remember in looking back, I believe that she finally returned his call twice. The first call was basically a courtesy or, quite possibly, her way of simply confirming her fear: That it was him. The second call, which came a week or so later, was not, in any way, what he expected.

After confirming that he was, in fact, the person calling, she had been subtly attempting to give him "the hint" by simply not returning the call. It was obvious that she was aware that he had been calling. But her issue was that he was too far gone. What she did not realize is that this physical transaction they had performed was not as simple as the world would lead us to believe. Most people fail to realize that the sexual relationship is just as spiritual in nature as it is physical. In fact, the spiritual influence may even outweigh the physical, especially under her circumstances...

I remember that he called me once to get my opinion on what was possibly going on. I had listened quietly over the weeks and watched his escalating indifference regarding this woman. He and I were close friends. So I decided to speak with him as candidly as we had become accustomed. I explained, "She used you." He couldn't grasp this concept so I expounded. I told him, "She is with someone else. I obviously can't tell you the nature of their relationship but part of the reason that she was so far gone sexually was possibly because she was hurting. You were merely a tool that was conveniently available at a time when she was vulnerable." He had difficulty accepting this.

The day finally came when she returned his call for the second and final time. From what he described, there was no small talk. She was cordial but brusque and direct. She began to explain that she was, in fact, "married," and that her husband had been away for some time serving an extended tour in the Middle East. He was in the military. She continued by telling him that the simple truth was that she was upset. She had been drinking that evening. She was lonely and missing him (meaning her husband), and my friend was, as I had previously attempted to explain, a convenient and "momentary" distraction from the pain she was suffering in her husband's absence. The problem is that she felt much worse afterwards than she did before she and my friend had shared in this intimate exchange. She expressed feeling horrible about using him but, even more so, for cheating on her husband. She told him that she had sworn afterwards never to subject herself, her husband, and their marriage, regardless of the circumstances, to such an act again. She apologized again, asked him politely but sternly NEVER to call her, ever, and abashedly ended the call, but not before apologizing once more.

This had only been a fleeting "moment" for her. But she deeply, viscerally regretted her decision. In that moment, she did not merely enter a physical exchange with my friend. There had been a spiritual intertwining as well, one that had been reserved exclusively for her "one" - her husband. She had unwittingly and unintentionally extended a spirit into her life, her husband's life, and the life of my friend that is designed to kill, steal, and destroy each one of their bodies, minds, and spirits, and their perfect union. She had taken her pure and "perfect love" and invited an element that should never have been given entry. As I've mentioned before, only one or the two of you harness the power to taint the perfectness that God establishes in your perfect love.

You would think that my friend would have been crushed. But, while for a moment he was disappointed, he, now completely delusional and in utter denial, concluded that he could change her mind. He attempted to contact her again. Honestly, just listening to him deteriorate so rapidly...this was all getting too weird even for me.

I can't remember if she simply did not call back or consequently changed her number. But in any event, he never spoke with her again. Thankfully, he did not have a last name or address to reference. I can only imagine the extent to which he may have gone if he had this information. Eventually though, this "spirit" receded, and he, my friend, finally got over it.

"Wisdom is the principal thing; therefore get wisdom: and with all thy getting get understanding. Exalt her, and she shall promote thee: she shall bring thee to honour, when thou dost embrace her. She shall give to thine head an ornament of grace: a crown of glory shall she deliver to thee." Proverbs 4:7-9.

Now, you may read this story and think that I may understand, practically justify, her decision for that evening considering the circumstances. If so, you are 100% WRONG! I do not condone or encourage this type of behavior, male or female, even under these circumstances. The marriage union is a commitment that is intended to be as eternal as Christ's love for the church, for better or for worse. Though I empathize and understand the loneliness factor, placing herself, firstly, into this position knowing, secondly, how vulnerable she was, how much she was hurting, and then, finally, the sex itself was simply...wrong. But the purpose of this story is not to bring light to her infidelity (that she deeply regretted). The focus is the unfortunate circumstances that disturbingly provoked her into dismissing her typical or normal sexual inhibitions or reservations, and inadvertently giving more of herself, in that moment, to this virtual stranger than she had ever given to her husband.

She explained to my friend in so many words that she did things with him that she had never done before. Yes, this was a common ploy of women who did not want to appear to be too "fast" back then. But even she explained that it was a combination of the alcohol (she wasn't a drinker), the hurt, and her loneliness that she was suffering in the absence of her husband. I elaborated further by explaining to him that she did not expect to ever see him again, and if she was going to "jump the fence" with him, she had decided to go "full in." Why hold back? To her, he was nothing but a tool. There was no real investment, or so she justified, so there was no reason to fear the loss of any real emotions. She did not care. But the truth is she had divested a part of the collective body of her and her husband's spiritual union to a complete stranger.

The interesting point to this is that her conduct, reasoning, and statements suggest that, as much as she expressed loving her husband, she was restraining herself sexually and the fullness of their experience together. Within the "perfect love," your husband or wife is divinely designated by God Himself to be the one person you are free to extend your all. You have the authority to enjoy each other to the maximum extent possible. Unfortunately in her case, she felt more open and uninhibited with a man that she did not love, or even "want" to love, than she did with her "one."

That is, in no way, what God intended for the two He created for one another. In fact, there are biblical references that clearly suggest that the two of you should enjoy each other so often, so freely, and so abundantly...that you should yearn for each other so eagerly...that the thought of being with anyone else is exhausting. Allow me to stress for the "religious" zealots out there, this does not negate walks in the park, catching a movie together, or simply calling to say "I love you." The fact is that all these acts nourish and constitute the marriage ministry. But the marriage ministry does not exclude, though some may be too religiously prissy to say it out loud, the sexual relationship.

"And God blessed them, and God said unto them, Be fruitful, and multiply, and replenish the earth, and subdue it (Genesis 1:28), "and whatsoever ye do, do it heartily." (Colossians 3:24).

It's almost comical how the Word has been twisted into supposedly separating what is appropriate and inappropriate inside of the marriage bed. But allow me to make something abundantly clear. When the Word refers to subjects surrounding "sexual immorality" or "immoral sexual conduct," the Word is quite specific regarding the areas that the writers were referring to at the time: (1) fornication (1 Cor. 6:18) and adultery (Prov. 6:32) - meaning sexual relations before, outside of, or apart from the marriage union; (2) sex with a prostitute or "harlot" (1 Cor. 6:15-16); and (3) homosexuality (Romans 1:26-27), specifically between men, though male gendered pronouns were often used by the writers to refer, generically, to both men and women.

The same holds true regarding your thoughts. While lusting after, "coveting," or desiring someone outside of your "one" is weighed as heavily as the commission of the actual act itself with that person or those people, it is not only right but is actually encouraged and expected for you to long for, desire, and even lust each other in Christ and within God's perfect love.

Much as in the story told, the woman's desperate desire or need to be with her husband is not sinful or wrong, and anyone who tells you otherwise is either delusional, attempting to paint a completely irrational facade, or is living in one really depressing household. While choosing to temporarily replace her husband was wrong, the longing for her "one" - her husband - is a longing for that very special part of God inside of her. And that's as innate as His love is for us.

Now, what about things such as oral and anal sex, and the like?

"The Word of God is not bound." (2 Timothy 2:9b).*"Utterance may be given unto me, that I may open my mouth boldly, to make known the mystery of the gospel, for which I am an ambassador in binds: that therein I may speak boldly, as I ought to speak."* (Ephesians 6:19-20).

The very first time that I heard a spiritual leader speak on this supposed "accursed" topic in a way that was inconsistent with "churchly" tradition yet perfectly in line with the Word itself was in the 90's in a convention where Bishop T.D. Jakes was both the facilitator and keynote speaker. It was through this convention that, for the very first time to my pseudo-religious, virgin ears, I actually watched a minister, Bishop Jakes accompanied boldly and proudly by his wife Serita, open the floor to questions by the audience and unexpectedly begin to discuss (or answer) a long awaited topic regarding fellatio and cunnilingus, or, for those unfamiliar with the more clinical terminology, the introduction and commission of oral sexual relations within a marriage. As he began to speak, it felt as if the entire place inhaled. Everyone was afraid to breathe or say anything that may, even slightly, divert attention from his address. Everyone in the audience was suddenly captivated by this forbidden question.

"Marriage is honourable in all, and the bed is undefiled." Hebrews 13:4.

There were the apparent uber-religious prudes - those men or women who are quick to condemn seemingly everything that could bring any real pleasure to your life while, behind the scenes, being more sexually explorative than any "missionary" could even attempt to placate. I love watching these individuals because the sad reality is that if their lives were as "reserved" and "restricted' as they may allude, they have truly missed a great deal of life and the world that God created for us to enjoy.

But also, in the audience were literally thousands instantly at the edge of their seat, men and women in God-filled and God-inspired relationships, people who actually lived their daily lives for Christ, that, though reluctant to pose the question themselves, were now quietly yet eagerly praying for the green light.

I don't remember Bishop Jakes' response verbatim, but I'll never forget his personal, Spirit-led conclusion. It was taken from the verse just mentioned. Bishop Jakes, in his eloquent way, summarized it by simply explaining that what goes on between a husband and a wife inside the privacy of their bedroom, or any area or location temporarily serving this purpose, is not only acceptable but, quite literally, a gift from God to each member of their perfect union. In other words, using a simpler and more contemporary vernacular to express his sentiment for husbands and wives forged together in God's perfect loving union in a marriage that is ordained by God Himself...it's okay to get your freak on!

"There is no fear in love. But perfect love drives out fear." 1 John 4:18.

Love, as in a "perfect love," has no limitations or set parameters. It should never be restricted to the ideas of someone outside of your union. Love is perfect when its foundation is vested exclusively in you and your "one" as established by God. A perfect love...your perfect love...is perfect when it is truly yours meaning the two of you alone. And if your love for one another is as unfettered and unrestrained as God intended, "naked and unashamed" in all things between the two of you, this is also as it should be in every intimacy that defines the experience, or the actual ministry, of the sexual relationship within your marriage.

Contrary to what others may attempt to lead you into believing, subscribing to, or accepting, the Word tells us that "Marriage is honourable in all things, and the bed undefiled." In love, God gave us dominion over ALL things. That includes, first and foremost, your loving union and the method in which the two of you find your greatest pleasure and pastime for nourishing and cultivating your "perfect love" through Christ.

There are no boundaries other than what the two of you decide upon, and it is no one else's business how vast or restrained the two of you assign to the ministry within your marriage. What I can tell you is that this part of the marriage is intended to be liberating. Remember that you are with "The One" - meaning that special individual whose every breath that you breathe and hold wonderfully inside of you, before anything else, is pure ecstasy and because the "perfect love" cannot be placated by just any physical replacement and erogenous act. A "perfect love" is, in fact, transcendent, reducing anything and anyone else aside or apart from "The One" to...nothing. That's because your connection to "The One" is a spiritual connection that is unmatched. In fact...it's God.

"*Be ye doers of the Word, and not hearers only.*" (James 1:12). Therefore, "*exhort one another daily, while it is called Today; as any of you be hardened through the deceitfulness of sin.*" (Hebrews 3:13).

And yes, if God has given the two of you the peace and passion, the yearning and desire for one another that includes oral and anal sexual inclinations, just as an example, that is acceptable before God Himself, regardless of what many may attempt to say.

"The bed is undefiled." This means that between a husband and his wife, divined by God, and filled by His "perfect love," the bed is pure and free from corruption; and every act within your bedroom is essentially a gift from the Creator Himself. It is intended for the wife to enjoy her husband as if his body was under her control. Likewise, it is intended for the husband to find pleasure in his wife as if her body was his to wield.

So, stop restraining yourselves from the dreams and desires that you have for one another. It's okay to be inventive and experimental because what you do is out of love and your need to bring her, or him, the greatest that God has placed inside of your bodies and your union to achieve. It is freeing because together you now have the confidence to be and to do everything to and with your "one." But there is a fundamental prerequisite: It's honesty.

"Take fast hold of instruction; let her not go: keep her, for she is thy life." Proverbs 4:13.

Part of the reason that this book was written and arranged in the order that it has been is because, for example, it was vital for you to be exposed to the concept and capable of rising to that level where you are completely "naked and unashamed." I needed you to understand that "getting naked and being unashamed," though you may be fully clothed in the physical sense, must be in all things surrounding you and your life. It is where all of you has been laid out on the metaphorical table and openly exposed to the other. But even this is not divinely intended just for anyone and everyone.

God created each one of us for a specific purpose: To complete the life of the "One" person that He created and designed just for you exclusively. And it is with that person that through Christ we are ultimately transformed into a new creation, together forming "one." It's through "The One" that we are perfected.

It is complete honesty that is the key to unlocking the door of unrestricted and unrestrained intimacy. This is what makes the greatest difference: It is when the two of you together expose all of yourselves to one another, and strangely, almost magically, the two are bonded, through Christ, into a single, new creation, loving each other, as impossibly as it may see, just that much more, infinitely, and eternally. It is when you find beauty in what she confides in you as her ugliness. It is when you love without condition perpetually. It is when you are somehow able to look past and forgive the unforgivable. It is accepting and adoring all of her, and she inherently accepting and adoring all of you. It transcends the physical beauty or deformity, the shapely or unshapely, the tall or the short, and the rich or the poor. It is the husband and his wife as seen, loved, created, and experienced by and through Christ that is the "perfect love."

"And be not conformed to this world but be ye transformed by the renewing of your mind, that ye may prove what is good, acceptable, and perfect, will of God." Romans 12:2.

To truly experience the divinity and perfection of the sexual bond or connection within the "perfect love" as husband and wife, each must be willing to disconnect himself and herself from everything that is of this world. What I mean by that is to enter this heavenly realm of pure and unadulterated ecstasy, the two of you must be willing to pour every part of yourselves, or invest every bit of your being, into each other. This covenant is meant to break you free from your believed faults, insecurities, the lies told in the past, the sins committed, the bills, the stresses, the problems, the worries, the complaints, and the past. Because in that moment, that beautiful, delicious moment, the two of you are a new creation, or reaffirming your singularity through Christ.

Many women are challenged with the inability to experience consistent or repeated orgasms. While there are those who may be diagnosed with physiological or biological conditions that preclude this from occurring, I have learned that for most women it's primarily predicated on a spiritual, psychological, and/or emotional impediment. Many women are literally mired inside and outside of the bedroom in known and unknown thoughts or burdens from the past or the present that impede or impair their ability to completely immerse themselves into the beauty, the passion, and the peace of this immaculate experience. But "being naked and completely unashamed" even before entering the bedroom assures that this is something that you should never, if ever, suffer when joined with your "one." Why? Because the power, protection, and purity formed out of your aggregate openness, honesty, commitment to each other, and unrestrained adoration for each other literally eviscerates this challenge. Fear and confusion are replaced with focus, respect, understanding, and compassion.

Remember that "getting naked and being unashamed" ensures that there is nothing between the two of you, mental, physical, emotional, or spiritual. His body is your body to enjoy, and your body is his to celebrate. It means that you are open to discussing and to trying sexual activities because you can do anything with that person. Why? Because he or she is "The One."

The body even reacts differently with "The One" because your heart, mind, and spirit are in a much different and higher place - a form of heaven, and an existence that the world cannot begin to fathom or intellectualize. Things taste and feel sweeter than anything that could ever be experienced before, apart from, or outside of "The One." There is harmony, balance, a pure, complete, and unadulterated love, and a perfect, perfect peace.

A question that some may ask: Is this supposed to be like this always where we long for each other insatiably? As I mentioned earlier in this book, when a man is preparing to die under the "perfect love" he will find himself longing for his wife's breath to be the very last that he breathes because throughout his lifetime, it is in and out of her that his entire being has been sustained.

The reality is that this should not be and, in a perfect love, is never a question that even requires asking. Within a "perfect love," she, or he, is your sustenance, and a desire that should be unyielding. So do not allow the world to dictate the limits of your ardency and affection for one another. In Christ, your love is eternal, your craving for one another voracious, and that is in whatever way or form that your ministry through Christ is so defined. It IS amazing though, within a "perfect love," how this happens to seem to fall right in line.

"Let every man have his own wife, and let every woman have her own husband. Let the husband render unto the wife due benevolence: and likewise also the wife unto the husband. The wife hath not power of her own body, but the husband: and likewise, also the husband hath not power of his own body, but the wife. Defraud ye not one the other, except it be with consent for a time, that ye may give yourselves to fasting and prayer; and come together again, that Satan tempt you not for your incontinency." 1 Corinthians 7:2b-5.

The Word instructs us to give ourselves to each other with "due benevolence." In other words, we should yield our bodies to one another often, openly, and excitedly, whenever we are physically capable, unless fasting and praying, or focusing on something for a time for the ultimate benefit of your union or family. But after this period passes, your thirst for one another - the husband and his wife - should be quenched as often as your body yearns.

Some women may be reading this and flippantly saying to themselves, "Of course, this is written by a man." Allow me to emphasize that, based on worldly stigmas that have corrupted our even believing in a "perfect love," I understand and empathize with your sentiment. But, by you thinking in such a manner, it

THE PERFECT LOVE BOOK

inadvertently calls into question whether the world or God's love is influencing the driving ministry in YOUR marriage.

Life should be fun and enjoyed, especially when you have been blessed to have been joined to your "one." It should be exciting, liberating, and yes, even adventurous, together. You can be daring, dominant or submissive. You can be "restrained." You can be acrobatic. But you also can be compassionate, gentle, lovingly, and tempestuously meticulous, taking your time, slowly and progressively building each moment, from a simmer to a stew.

Together, you should laugh as often and as affectionately as you love one another. Contrary to what some may think, the marriage ministry is not exclusive to the pleasure of the man or husband, but rather is designed to be consonant acts of reciprocity, where you long to do to and to do for each other as God places upon your heart in loving one another, wholly and completely.

Women, it is not just about him, but also about you. In fact, the love that he expends in or connects to you through Christ, that "perfect love," that will, quite often, inspire him to seek what you may discover is actually his greatest pleasure, which is to ensure that YOU are aware that you, and you alone, are unequivocally his only focus, and that your joy, happiness, excitement, and ecstasy is achieved even before his own, or, fantastically, together.

But this ministry is not limited to the confines of the bedroom or even to conventional intercourse. Love making, or the perfect love in the marriage ministry, is knowing with absolute certainty that he or she loves you, meaning all of you, wholly and completely. That she, or he, will never forsake you or the gift that is your union. It's understanding that the "One" was formed and framed by God Himself for you. "The One" is the greatest gift given by the Creator because she or he is your perfection, and in that "perfect love" is forever your protection.

The marriage ministry, or love making, is often just as simple as being able to stare into and drink from the pools of your wife's beautiful eyes. It is experiencing the way her hand feels and contours to your own. It is in the ability to breathe the breath that she exhales as she speaks, and the rush of excitement and emotion as her breath warms your skin. You will find yourself enchanted and enthralled simply by her smile, and ecstasy begins whenever the "One" walks into the room. It is a sensual and spiritual experience merely thinking about the way their lips...their nose...their ears are formed and framed, or watching the rise and fall of one's chest because in the evidence of her existence, you are given and continue to experience life as God truly intended.

Men, causing her to laugh or to ponder over a thought that you may have intimated should be exhaustively erogenous. Hearing the excitement in her voice about...anything...is deliciously enticing. But these things affect us in this way NOT because she is simply a woman. She affects every part of our being because she is your "one" - the greatest and most wonderful gift that God has ever given to man and whom you should honor most in everything and anything that constitutes her being. Why? Because she is physical evidence of God's literal existence and His unbelievable love for you.

There are no limitations within the ministry that God has placed in us. A "perfect love" is whole and perfect, and emblematic of the pure beauty of "The One" and in being "naked and unashamed." No limitations. No restrictions. No fear. Just love...the perfect love...between the two of you in Christ.

"Enjoy life with your wife whom you love and with your children, family and friends as long as you live. Life by itself is a meaningless round of activities, and without some happiness it's not worth living. Whatever you do, do your best and enjoy it." Ecclesiastes 9:9-10 (Clear Word).

Men, understand that part of your responsibility in protecting your wife, your "one," is to appreciate her and her brilliance, and the magnitude of her being. But the Word also tells us that it is to ensure that she is extended all your heart, mind, spirit, body, passion, and compassion. It is your responsibility to create an atmosphere where she can be her whole, true, and complete self; where she can speak with you openly and honestly; and where she can make suggestions without fear of being criticized, embarrassed, or castigated. It is through you that she should be elevated to such a level of comfort, truth and honesty, respect, and peace, which empowers her with the ability to transform into and to experience the excitement in being as wonderful as God created her. Your greatest pleasure should be to usher her to a place where her pleasure is prominent and paramount. She is your "crown of glory" and your perfection.

Women, know that it is acceptable by God Himself to enjoy your husband wholly and completely. Remember that you are God's greatest gift to your husband, perfect and undefiled. Love and enjoy the things that you do as your heart so desires with your "One" because that is as God intended. The world may call it "freaky," but, in Christ, it's one of the most beautiful expressions of the perfect love and the ministry of your marriage.

"Lie not to one another, seeing that ye have put off the old man with his deeds; and have put on the new man, which is renewed in knowledge after the image of Him that created him." Colossians 3:9-10.

And finally, do not lie to one another. Dishonest is certain to taint His intended perfectness between the two of you. Lies are weapons of the enemy designed to impair or completely destroy your union. This infection is often fatal but it does not have to be.

Contrary to what you may feel or otherwise want to believe, a lie does not necessarily connote that he, or she, is suddenly no longer your "One." The two of you have been empowered with the ability to defeat the enemy together. The reality is that "The One" was, is, and will always be "The One," and no force on earth or in hell has the power to alter this fact.

The way to defeat this if it occurs inside of your union is to, first, apologize and expose the truth for whatever it may be. Remember that you are not speaking with just anyone. You are addressing "The One" who God designed for or from out of you. I am not going to suggest that it may not take a moment for a wound to heal, but, likewise, I am not going to denounce the instant healing power of Christ. This is not about what neighbors or friends may say, or even what family might think. It is singularly about the two of you and the Father. It's about your perfect love and the realization that she, or he, is "The One." It's about loving her, or him, as perpetually as Christ loves the church, and dying daily, and with each day, renewing your commitment, transforming into that new creation in Christ. It's about God and appreciating the gift that He has given you in "The One."

But it is also, in love, calling forth the confidence and compassion to let the past, even the lies, go; recognizing that tomorrow is a new day; and together you have been given a new opportunity.

This does not justify the lie at all. The person who lies should recommit sincerely in that moment to never allowing that spirit to enter your perfect union again. One of the most effective tools in distracting us from achieving the goodness, the greatness, and the grace of the profound intimacy of the marriage ministry is a lie. Remember that honesty in ALL things is the key. But if asks sincerely within a perfect love to forgive, forgive just as Christ does for us. Be as Christ and have the audacity to trust Him to trust her, or him, and to let it go. And I assure you that when you do, God's got something much greater for the two of you: It's called life.

You see, real fear is when you think you may have lost "The One." Don't get me wrong. It may not be about a lie or infidelity. It could be something simpler, or possibly more complex, than that. The worst is when you are trying to disregard what God has revealed as clear as day: This is the "One." Yes, I understand. Your greatest fear begins and ends simply in the thought of losing the "One." In times of doubt or fear, the question is what to do...

CHAPTER SEVEN
WHEN YOU THINK YOU'VE LOST "THE ONE"

When You Think You've Lost "The One"

When you think that you've lost "The One," it feels as if a vital part of your being has been surgically removed or has been suddenly altered from its natural state and for some reason you can't remember when it all took place. This emptiness. This void. Thinking that you have lost "The One" is definitively different from thinking that you have suddenly lost anyone or anything else. For those people who have never experienced losing "The One,' it's an impression that stroked much deeper than common heart break, and more profoundly than mere loneliness. It is unlike when you sunder from anyone else because even in her or his physical absence, an underlying bond or knowing spirit subtly, quietly endures. In fact, there's a forbidden and secret "hope" or "faith" that almost tells you...maybe...just maybe...because "no man CAN put asunder."

As I mentioned previously, being "The One" does not mean that "The One" cannot become involved in another relationship. But becoming involved with someone else or relocating to the other side of the earth for that matter does not change the truth in "The One" being your only "one" under God. It may be a distraction. It may even be something that you are able to suppress on some conscious level. You may even be able to convince yourself that she or he "probably" was not "The One," at least for a moment. But deep within your subconscious, you know better. Your spirit dreams of closure and completion. It longs to be whole again. It aspires to achieve that level of peace, grace, prosperity, joy, and love that only "The One" is capable of facilitating.

I would imagine that the thought of losing "The One" is much like having an arm or leg amputated; a part of you that regardless of the passing of time always feels and appears somewhat unnatural because being whole is about possessing every member of your natural, God given body. This is not to suggest that a person born without a limb or who has a limb removed is unnatural or its absence unassailable. I am blessed to still have all my limbs intact. So, I cannot speak from experience with respect to actual amputation of a limb. This analogy though is simply to illustrate the innate expectation and spiritual implication that "The One" imbues throughout your entire body simply in being a supernatural, God-infused part of your holier existence.

When you think that you've lost The One, your life just seems empty. A person that I once spoke with told me that when he thought that he had lost his "one," it felt as if a hole had been burrowed into his chest but instead of simply dying, he was forced to live with this tremendous opening running through him. But, here's something to consider. There's a reason that it feels like this.

"For this reason a man will leave his mother and father and be united to his wife, and they will become one flesh." Genesis 2:24.

When a man is born, he is born lacking a part of what God intended for him to possess to make himself whole. In the story of Adam and Eve, it was simply referred to as Adam's rib, out of which Eve was subsequently created. Remember that God removed just a single rib and ultimately created an entire beautiful being designed to perfect his greatest work of creation in Adam. There was nothing greater or otherwise required once Eve was coupled to Adam because at that point, the Creator had achieved perfection through their union.

Think about the fact that these two - the husband and his wife - were created from one body of work to form a Godly masterpiece. He extracted a part of Adam's own body and created Eve who exemplifies the perfecting of Adam. That is "The One."

"Now faith is being sure of what we hope for and certain of what we do not see." Hebrews 11:1.

When I said that it is about faith, it is about understanding, knowing, and then accepting what God has given the two of you in each other. I stress "the two of you" because that oneness, wholeness, and utter perfection requires you and her, or him, to take form. "The One" is as vital to your divine conjugation as you are to theirs. It's when "the two" recognize the beauty within their amalgamated existence that forms the foundation for appreciating your new life as a singular, new creation in Christ.

And it can be daunting. In fact, it can be downright scary and intimidating. I've seen people run from the Spirit because of the completely new and foreign effect that it has on your entire life. I've heard of others living a lifetime of denial, refusing to accept what every molecule making up every morsel of their body has inadvertently confirmed. This is because when you decide to allow the Spirit entry into your life it's as nothing that an inexperienced person or a person who has not been enlightened, not merely by hearing the Word but actually living in that Word, could begin to envisage.

"But Jesus turned about and when He saw her, he said, Daughter, be of good comfort; thy faith hath made thee whole. And the woman was made whole from that hour." Matthew 9:22.

It requires faith in a force that, at first, may be difficult for you to understand or grasp. It's faith in someone that is much greater than the two of you individually. It's having faith in the substance of what He has established between the two of you; faith that recognizes the unbreakable and impermeable bond that He has forged and framed through your union. It's faith that only faith can control. It's accepting the understanding and knowing that through her, or him, you have been perfected in Christ just in your spouse being suddenly present in your life.

I have learned that even when you think you have lost "The One" forever, continue to hold fast to the profession of your faith in Him, "for He is faithful that promised." (Heb. 10:23). If you are willing to trust Him, trust Him completely. Inevitably, He will satisfy your heart and spiritual need and desire for your "one." It may not be easy. At times, it may even get frustrating. But allow Him to guide you to that place of peace in "The One." When you decide to allow the Spirit entry into your life, it's as nothing that an inexperienced person or a person who has not been enlightened, not merely by hearing the Word but actually living in that Word, could begin to envisage.

"But Jesus turned about and when He saw her, he said, Daughter, be of good comfort; thy faith hath made thee whole. And the woman was made whole from that hour." Matthew 9:22.

It requires faith in a force that, at first, may be difficult for you to understand or grasp. It's faith in someone that is much greater than the two of you individually. It's having faith in the substance of what He has established between the two of you; faith that recognizes the unbreakable and impermeable bond that He has forged and framed through your union. It's faith that only faith can control. It's accepting the understanding and knowing that through her, or him, you have been perfected in Christ just in her, or his, being suddenly present in your life.

I have learned that even when you think you have lost The One forever, continue to hold fast to the profession of your faith in Him, "for He is faithful that promised." (Heb. 10:23). If you are willing to trust Him, trust Him completely. Inevitably, He will satisfy your heart and spiritual need and desire for your "one." I can attest to the truth of this fact. It may not be easy. At times, it may even get frustrating. But allow Him to guide you into the direction that will lead you back on the path to finding your perfection.

"Come to me, all you who are weary and burdened and I will give you rest. Take my yoke upon you and learn from me, for I am gentle and humble in heart, and you will find rest for your souls. For my yoke is easy and my burden is light." Matthew 11:28-30 (Clear Word).

There's a passage that is often referred to but just as often grossly misinterpreted or misconstrued in its misinterpretation, and in doing so causing an elemental point to be consequently misapprehended. It reads, "I can do all things through Christ which strengtheneth me." (Philippians 4:13). Many people read this as the ultimate profession of infinite ability to achieve the utterly impossible, which, through Christ, you have been given this ability. BUT... Within the meaning of this particular scripture and the surrounding remarks, this has been taken slightly out of context.

If you read the preceding 2 verses alone you will discover that this verse actually refers to your personal outlook or perspective despite your status or position or stature in one moment of your life compared to the next. Making this a little more relatable with respect to "The One," when you are with "The One" or when you think that you have lost "The One," as long as you are able to maintain your focus on the prize as well as your faith in His power to fulfill His promise, regardless of the stage you may find yourself in with respect to "The One" - meaning going into, coming out of, or regaining your "perfect love" with "The One," you will make it through to the ending point that He has always intended for you to arrive at within the "perfect love." The more that you trust Him and let go, the greater the peace you will experience.

When you think you've lost The One, trust Him to guide you to making things whole again. That cannot be achieved by being a nuisance or a nightmare, but rather by nurturing your faith in Him. That is what will eventually make you whole again.

In the interim, use this time to reassess and redefine your mode of thinking. Take a moment to recollect the strength and unfathomable joy infused into every part of your being just from the mere thought of her, or his, smile or a subtle moment shared together. Respect and practice expressing and showing your gratefulness for the perfectness that God established in you through

"The One." Recognize her, or his, greatness through Christ. And work to envision the infinite, wonderful possibilities that He has set up for the two of you to experience together. Replace your fear with faith in and focus on God's "perfect love" for your adoring union.

Given another opportunity, make certain that not a day will go by that you fail to encourage "The One" or to do all that you can to build that person up and to help "The One" understand how special he or she is. Openly and affectionately confess your love for your "One" daily as if it was the first day of the rest of your new life together because in each day that you are given another opportunity to enjoy and celebrate your "One", recognize that you are the most fortunate person on God's green earth. At least that's how He makes you feel through "The One."

Every day that you are given the opportunity to have and to love one another, revel in that day as if starting over with "The One" for the very first time. The difference being, now you know. And for those who don't know what it is to start over or what to expect when starting over with "The One," allow me to paint this beautiful picture for you.

CHAPTER EIGHT
STARTING OVER WITH "THE ONE"

N. D. "Indy" Brennan

Starting Over With "The One"

Imagine waking up every morning to an absolutely perfect partner in a completely perfect world, where in the midst of what others would deem devastating, you continue to celebrate the infinite opportunities that are instantly extended to the two of you to experience together and enjoy. Starting over with "The One" means that from the first day to the next, you are given a new chance to experience the perfection of God's grace and love for you because your "One" symbolizes your entire everything coming full circle. The mere knowledge of her or his existence resolves your perfection. Your life resembles something that others may deem unrealistic, but the fact is that what the two of you have become, worldly men, or women for that matter, will never truly understand unless revealed through God and exposed to His "perfect love" in their life.

Your divine union with "The One" defines God's greatest greatness for your life. Meditate on the fact that once He completed the creation and spiritual fusion of Adam and Eve, His work in their creation was so awesome that even he stepped back, admiring the impeccable work of His own hand, and rested.

Perfect means that there is nothing else that needs to be done or said. A perfect love is one without "spot or wrinkle...holy and unblemished." (Ephesians 5:27). In a "perfect love" there is "no fear" (1 John 4:18), and you may confidently "get naked and be

N. D. "Indy" Brennan

completely unashamed" (Genesis 2:25) because where your love is truly the "perfect love" then the essence of that love between you and your "One" flows from out of one source, and that's God. (1 John 4:16).

"We are only jars of clay, filled with the treasures of the gospel to show that its power is from God and not from us. Everywhere we go, we have trouble, but we're not discouraged. We're perplexed, but not confused. We're persecuted, but never abandoned. We're struck down, but not destroyed. We have faced death for the Lord Jesus many times and the scars on our bodies show it, but we are still alive, which testified to the power of Christ to deliver...So while death stalks us everywhere, new life is working in you!" 2 Corinthians 4:7-12 (Clear Word).

Starting over means that you have been elevated to a higher place. The wife is instantly "undefiled." The husband has regained his "crown" (Proverb 12:4), a "good thing" which reflects his "favour of the Lord." (Proverbs 18:22). He loves her as he loves his own body, which is reflective of Christ's love for the church. (Ephesians 5:25). She honors and respect her husband in accordance with the perfect will of Christ. (Ephesians 5:22). In her is your every love requirement both predicated and instantly demonstrated.

And through "The One," dare I say it, but your every sexual need and fantasy for one another, inspired and influenced by your "perfect love," is compelled to be experienced and fulfilled. For "The One" is the only "one" that you share in this personal, beautiful ministry. By starting over with "The One," you recommit to being completely honest and forthcoming in all things because this is an elemental prerequisite to sharing your most intimate secrets and sexual inclinations. "The One" trust you and desires to be everything for and to you. And it's okay to desire or even lust after "The One" continually, because this is part of the wonderful gift that God has endowed you with in your husband or your wife. The fact is, it is not only acceptable but actually expected.

Starting over with "The One" should be a celebration of life. I encourage you to be the complete man or woman, that husband or that wife, that God created for you to be for "The One." Honor her and respect him. Be there for each other and enjoy every moment that you are blessed to have one another in your life.

It is my hope and prayer that this book encourages you to seek even greater substance in your union. God is the key to your perfect love. All that you have to do is trust Him, and someday, inevitably, you may experience a perfect love in and with "The One." Selah.

Full Disclosure

When does "The One" become your wife? A wife is not determined by a piece of paper, the cut or clarity of the diamond, or the capacity of the audience observing the ritual ceremony in church. A wife becomes your wife not by the recitation of nuptials, jumping over a broom, or the filing of the marriage license. A wife becomes your wife not by man, but rather by God. Your eternal bond to each other is created long before the proposal is ever made. The bond between a husband and his wife is created by the Holy Spirit and out of what is professed and confirmed in the heart of that woman in Christ for her husband under God whose heart she is purposed to protect. Your wife, or your "one," is and has always been a part of your entire being, and this was made eternal long before your natural bodies existed and the two of you required air to breathe.

I have often thought about the love that God has for us. Regardless of how we may fail to reach out to Him and regardless of whatever we may do, I understand that He has never left me or forsaken me. The love and patience that God has for us is boundless and unmatched. He sees the very best and the worst of us yet He continues to love us still. Every day of our life, he shows us His perfect love for us. He is our greatest example.

I am no different from many of you regarding wanting to see things my way at times perhaps because God's way may not have been moving as quickly as I thought it should. I've made decisions that I found myself attributing to being of God when it was absolutely me. And I've engaged in past relationships when He did all but yell for me to run and found myself paying for that decision for decades afterwards. Even though we have ignored Him or acted to the contrary, He has never given up on us. Why? Because God's love is perfect.

Irrespective of anything I have ever done or been through, I realized that God's Word is true. So, if this book sounds too fantastic for you, I'd like for you to consider this. You may be of the mindset that a "perfect love" is impossible. You may consider the love that God has for us as something that can only be provided by God Himself, and that's okay. I totally and completely understand. When I was in my early 20's, my grandmother used to say, "You can't find a good girl out in those streets or clubs." Yet, she felt like I somehow did not fit into that mold even though I was hanging in those same street and dancing in those same clubs. This is the same mentality that many of us use when it comes to the "perfect love." You may be saying to yourself, "No one is capable of loving anyone like that," even though this is something you would love to share with someone. Consider this: If you are someone who is willing to give that of themselves to someone else, do you really believe you are the only one in the world who'd be willing or who desires to do the same?

There's one key to a perfect love that I failed to mention within this book but that we have beyond measure. It's that in order for love to truly be perfect, that love must be equal in its breadth and its distribution between the two of you. A perfect love equates to a divine balance, and it is within that equilateral affection of heart, body, and spirit that we find a peace beyond a mundane parochial understanding. This is what God has established for us to enjoy. The beauty described and defined by the brilliance of who another person is in your life through Christ and in this book will hopefully assist you in reaching that Garden of Eden God has waiting for you through your "one."

ABOUT THE AUTHOR

N D. Brennan is the author of "The Top 51 Business Hacks for 2021" and co-author of "What If White People Were Slaves?". He is also the live event coordinator and senior digital marketing executive for MADDCity.Live, LLC., a published author of other books, poetry, and commercial blogs, and the creator and co-host of The Book Slam on Clubhouse. He is an Internet entrepreneur and digital visionary with more than a 20-year history in social media marketing, I.T., and telecommunications. He is a professional copywriter, digital sales and marketing trainer, motivational speaker, and activist with an extensive background in commercial music and video production, and songwriting. He has worked as a leader, creative director, and within an entrepreneurial capacity with ventures involving Fortune 500 companies to Internet start-ups. For more information about the author and upcoming events, go to shop.ndbrennan.com, or email him at ndbrennanauthor@gmail.com. Follow the author on Instagram @nbrennanauthor.

www.ingramcontent.com/pod-product-compliance
Lightning Source LLC
Chambersburg PA
CBHW051653120626
46551CB00020B/1204